OVERLIVE

OVERLIVE

Power, Poverty, and the University

WILLIAM M. BIRENBAUM

 A Delta Book

A DELTA BOOK
Published by Dell Publishing Co., Inc.
750 Third Avenue
New York, N.Y. 10017

Delta ® TM 755118, Dell Publishing Co., Inc.
The hardcover edition of this book is published
by Delacorte Press, New York, N.Y.
Library of Congress Catalog Number: 68-9267
Manufactured in the United States of America

Second Delta Printing

To the students at
The Brooklyn Center
of Long Island University,
September, 1964 through
April, 1967

Contents

Preface

I HAVE taught at the University of Chicago, Wayne State University, the New School for Social Research, Long Island University, a neighborhood "college" in Bedford-Stuyvesant in Brooklyn, and at other foreign places, abroad. I have been a dean of students, the dean of a college, and a university vice-president and provost. I have occupied these positions and exercised the powers attending them most of my professional life.

I have been a part of what this book is about. What I have to say enjoys the advantage of firsthand experience and suffers from the engagement and commitment getting that experience required.

I was a university student once.

Some of my friends now in college tell me that it is impossible to have been a part of the Establishment as I have been and still keep the faith, still remain an honest agent for change and reform. And I have replied, acknowledging that power certainly does corrupt, that the possession and exercise of power (and the assumption of its responsibilities) is one way to bring about change—an alternative still, I think, to action in the streets or dropping out. But my friends may be right. I hope I am.

I am the father of three young people who have already learned a lot in spite of every school they have been in.

Even now they are learning more though they have yet to reach college age. I envy them for what they know, and I sympathize with the parents of the world in our mutual and colossal ignorance.

Not all parents have chosen careers in higher education. I hope that a few who haven't may benefit from what I "know" and have written down in this book. All of us could use an elementary course in how to improve our conversation with our offspring. This book may not be such a course, but it may serve to remind us that we need one.

I have found that the best way to handle the Generation Gap is to ignore it. It may be, probably is there. But I feel better acting as if it isn't. My children tell me that this sometimes leads to absurd conduct, but my absurdities make them laugh, which is not all bad.

Some of the youngest, most vigorous people I know are over seventy. Horace M. Kallen, who is over eighty-five, is one of these. Saul Bloch, who is over seventy-five, is another. Both of these men are great teachers because they never stopped learning. They understand what's going on almost as well as many of the concerned students I admire so much. These two men (and many of the students) inspired and helped me along the way of writing this book.

I have lived most of my adult life in Chicago, Detroit, and New York. Two of these places are cities, and the third really ought to be.

I like cities. I think most young adults ought to go to college in a city, if they should go to college at all. So many people I know don't like cities, except as places to visit occasionally. So many people I know live in cities. It's really very sad—living in cities and not liking them except as places to visit occasionally.

I believe that the experience of being in a city and of it is an essential part of the higher learning now. An idea similar to this once occurred to some Greeks. But I was born in a small town in Illinois and received my lower education in Iowa. Iowa is closer to New York than it is to Athens, but it's a long way from both. Most of the people going to college these days were not born and raised in small towns or places like Iowa. Most of them will not settle down in such places—charming as they really are. I hope that more people will come to like living in cities, because that's where they're going to live. The will to learn is strengthened when people enjoy living where they learn. It helps to feel at home at home, which is not how most people feel on campus.

I began writing this book before the students on the campus where I was went on strike in April of 1967. Most of their faculty and many people in the surrounding Brooklyn communities supported the students' strike. They respected the picket lines and many joined them. The students struck because I was "invited" to resign. Ideas discussed in this book were involved in the invitation I got. The students and many of the faculty members who were a part of those events learned something new they will not soon forget. The strike failed, but so did the subsequent attempt by the trustees to solve their problems by selling the campus, lock, stock, and barrel.

I finished this book B.C.—Before Columbia happened, in April of 1968. Meantime and since many hopeful things have occurred along with the usual flow of dreary and distressing academic events. Special scholarship programs for black students have become fashionable. Curricula are beginning to display black subjects in their front windows. University presidents are making speeches about the new responsibilities of their institutions in the urban "crisis." Trustees are making announcements that some changes should be made. There are pleas for faculties to pay some attention to what they're doing. Almost every urban school has hired or is desperately trying to hire at least one black administrator. At least one men's school in New England has even announced that it's going to admit women.

The idea of a university as a community devoted to learning is something I deeply respect. And I am a born optimist. More such places really could be. But I don't believe what's bothering us can be fixed up with Scotch tape.

Abraham I. Habenstreit, with whom I have been associated since joining the staff of Long Island University in 1964, has been a sensitive and important reader of this work. He brought to it the advantage of having been suspended once for his editorship of the student newspaper at City College in New York.

I am indebted to my colleagues in The Education Affiliate in Bedford-Stuyvesant for their tutelage. Most of them have either been suspended from something at least once, or are in suspense.

There are many students and nonstudents of many different colors and persuasions in and about New York, Chicago, Detroit, Boston, Syracuse, Ithaca, Madison, Stanford, New Haven, Berkeley and elsewhere to whom I am indebted. They have argued, drunk, eaten, sat-in and done other helpful things with me that members of minority groups tend to do with each other.

Patricia Parsons, my administrative assistant, has aided and abetted this book from beginning to end, and I am grateful to her.

Finally, I must acknowledge my wife's contribution to this work. I met her in a classroom at the University of Chicago, and she's seen me through many wars. Though she is a member of the academic profession, she is not an "academic wife." She has been this book's severest critic (so far), but without her encouragement and help I may not have taken the risks of putting down what I think at this particular point in my experience.

WILLIAM M. BIRENBAUM

New York City
May 1968

OVERLIVE

1

Overlive

One of the terms that has come to be accepted in the vocabulary of military leaders is the "overkill factor." It denotes surplus killing power, expressed in the ratio between what is actually available for use against a population target and what would be necessary as a minimum to destroy it. In the spring of 1960 each of the two Great Powers was reported to have an atomic stockpile capable of killing every man, woman, and child in the world many times over.

MAX LERNER[1]

WE AMERICANS have always assumed that working solutions to most of our problems exist. All we need do is look for and discover them. This optimistic outlook is a part of our charm and a major source of our national success.

The country has had good reason to be confident. Its technology is first. Everywhere in the world the U.S. is known for its know-how, its ability to organize and to get things done. The U.S. produces more goods for more people than any country has ever produced. The great majority of Americans enjoy the highest standard of living ever known among such a large population. This success encourages even greater expectations. Our economy depends upon the faith of the majority in the limitless power to produce even more, and in the validity of each citizen's possession of an ever greater share of the production.

But while the majority profess this faith, deep and disturbing blemishes mark the quality and meaning, the tone and spirit of national life. The power to live "well" has generated widespread feelings of powerlessness. The superior technology, the urban concentration of people resulting from it, and the organizational schemes we have invented to manage and control ourselves, all raise the most serious questions about the original values guiding the country's growth. Somehow, neither the fruits of the technology nor the organizational inventiveness seem to provide adequate responses to the questions they raise. Not since the Civil War have so many Americans been embattled with their fellow Americans. The battlegrounds are the American meanings of Freedom, Equality of Opportunity, Free Enterprise, and Peace.

There are two thrusts to the promise of the traditional American Way. One is the possibility of *producing* sufficient goods and services to enable all of our people to enjoy a standard of living conducive to meaningful participation in our versions of Freedom and Equality of Opportunity. The other is the operation of ground rules in law, social custom, and practice which lead to and maintain an effective *distribution* and use of the goods and services. The American credo is "The opportunities are great and everyone has access to them." As a result of the pursuit of the opportunities, everyone will end up being better off.

For many Americans things don't seem to be working out this way. The productive capacity at last seems possible. But the success has become colored and distorted by an *overlive factor*. Overlive is the nonmilitary counterpart of overkill—*a surplus living power, expressed in the ratio between the capacity of the country to produce in the fulfillment of the promises it makes to all of its people, and what it actually produces and does with its great power.*

We have created an overlive society—*a country in which*

*a substantial number of the citizens do not share in the
technological and industrial success which is there for all
to see; and in which many of those who do, fail to discover
any meaning in the success.*

Overlive as a way of life and overkill as a policy for making that way secure grow from the same roots. One is the
inevitable complement of the other. American product-
inventiveness and productive capacity make the overkill
approach to national security possible. The most serious
problems in this approach do not arise out of the difficulties
of *producing* the bombs. They have to do with making
decisions about the *distribution* of the products (bombs).

> . . . The great powers, with their enormous margin for over-
> kill, have far more power than they can or dare use without
> risking their own destruction. They are caught in the paradox
> of their own excess killing power.[2]

The goal of the tremendous overkill production effort is
the *non*use, the *non*distribution of the goods. Only if the
policy fails does overkill move to saturate the market (enemy
territory) with the products (bombs) through a distribution
system and effort so massive that the destruction of both
the consumer (the enemy) and the producer-seller (us) is
insured.

At the heart of the overkill policy is a deep faith in an
extraordinary capacity to produce the goods and in the mere
possession of a great surplus. According to this faith, disaster
is deterred by the power to produce. People optimistic about
this deterrent principle get little comfort from history. History is full of examples of men and groups ready, willing,
and able to take on the impossible odds. There has never
been a very long shortage of first-strikers. Another's superior
power to produce often tempts the underdog to strike first.

History notwithstanding, the overkill approach to problem
solving is very appealing to those who have or want to have

faith in the traditional American Way. It capitalizes upon the existence of surpluses Americans have always assumed they have—of time, space, and treasure. It assumes the wisdom of overproducing and storing wheat and corn for rainy days—bombs for the days of their possible reign. It relies upon those very qualities Americans believe they are most famous for—the know-how, the organizational genius, the ability to produce the goods. Overkill exemplifies a principle always attractive to Americans: Confronted with an extremely complicated situation, doing something is better than doing nothing, especially if the "something" exploits doing what we are supposed to do best.

Fortunately, the American people do not daily have to decide whether to use the bomb. Their daily decisions concern such things as making a living, maintaining familial peace, getting educated, walking down city streets, and being "American." These are often tough decisions. They are tough when it's impossible to make a living, or when making a living involves doing things which are dull, unpleasant, or dehumanizing; or when it may not be safe to walk down the street; or when it is not at all clear how to go about being "American." In faraway places, on the streets in the very centers of our greatest cities, and behind the comfortable façade of suburbia, the context for making these decisions has become explosive.

Overkill is one formulation of what to do with power on the occasion of an unusual collision between politics, economics, and technology. Overlive, too, is a power crisis. It is a crisis born not from the lack, but because of an excess of power and a strange incapacity to use what we have where it counts. In the black ghettos American power has not served to cool the situation; quite the opposite, it has operated like a giant lens to magnify the heat of injustice felt by those who are powerless. In the middle-class suburbs American power has not served to shift the emphasis from acquiring things to the perfection of life goals; quite the opposite, it has produced time and value vacuums and a compulsive drive to fill the voids with more things. Abroad, American power has not served to achieve results desired or to earn the respect of others; quite the opposite, it has led to frustration, waste, and degradation.

Frustration in the use of American power has created an obsession with the maintenance and expansion of the capacity to produce more. To each of the explosive problems of distribution, the main response is to produce more. And the mere production of more in overlive's terms tends to aggravate the problems of distribution and use. The greater the overlive production, the more incendiary the situation threatens to become. The goals promised by the American Way heighten the sense of dilemma. The most pressing problems of the country call for the engagement of all the power we possess, and probably of even more yet to be produced. But overlive productive capacities are now seldom fully mobilized; they have yet to surmount the hard political and social barriers to the solution of those key problems which, left unsolved, threaten the whole system.

In its obsession with the productive capacity, the overlive economy makes consumption a function of production needs rather than production a function of consumer needs. It plans obsolescence. It encourages the acceptance of products that wear out quickly and require frequent replacement; or it introduces a never-ending stream of product variations, innovations on basic designs that induce the consumers to replace working products with more "modern," up-to-date versions. It imposes the principle of obsolescence alike upon those who can afford it and the poor, who cannot. The act of consuming is paramount to the satisfaction of the actual consumer needs. In fact, consumption is often promoted at the expense of consumer health, as the campaigns to sell many drugs and tobaccos illustrate.

One of the officially proclaimed payoffs for the overlive economy is the enrichment of the variety and quantity of human experience. The number of different cars, cereals, colleges, books, and amusement alternatives available to potential consumers is greatly increased. At the same time, the number of producers diminishes. Fewer decision-making centers direct the production of an increasing number of things. The efforts of the producers to individualize their products are vigorous and command a large portion of the competitive energy expended in selling. The imperatives of saturation, obsolescence, and the voguishness of trying something new conceal the sameness embodied in the alternatives. Choice, if there is any at all, occurs among alternatives so numerous and indistinguishable as to blur reasonable perception, as the speed of a vehicle blurs a view of the countryside for its passengers.

For example, the overlive economy puts television—a machine through which the viewers' experience may readily be extended and potentially diversified—into the homes of the masses. It then standardizes and homogenizes their choice by the similarity of the programs offered to them. In the purchase of the machines, consumers are offered a wide range of alternatives basically alike in style, durability, and price. The illusion of significant choice is underscored by a frantic competition to sell.

The purchaser of a college education, in many respects, is in exactly the same position as the purchaser of a television set—with regard to both the product (the college) and the transmissions (the educational programs). Since the beginning of the Vietnam war new colleges have been opening in the United States at the rate of almost one a week. Each claims to offer the latest, unique push-button approach, the most ingenious and foolproof system for dialing in instant, clear-vision, wide-screen learning. In fact, each is almost indistinguishable from the others, and all are essentially replications of the older models. There may be some quality variance among the parts used, but the designs, styles, and programming are basically the same.

Action and motion are the central themes in the overlive society. The wheel is its emblem—or the escalator. Everyone seems to be going somewhere other than where he is—hopefully, up. The technology encourages him to think that he can go. The economy promises to equip him to go. The language of politics underscores the respectability of going. The psychological environment says that, if he doesn't go, there is something wrong with him. Overlive is go-go.

Huge pumping stations dominate the overlive countryside, producing the gigantic supplies of energy, the driving forces for the motion. The pumps include labor unions, poverty programs, educational institutions, progressive income taxation, the stockmarket, suburban shopping centers, the substitution of credit for money, and the extension of insurance security principles into almost every aspect of human existence.

Often the main purpose of the motion is simply the consumption of the energy which makes it possible. The official rationale for the motion is progress. The act of going is often confused with the fact of getting somewhere. But much of the motion is planned to be wasted and, through the waste, defeats progress. If it were not wasted, the foundations of the overlive economic structure—product saturation, obsolescence, and innovation—would be undermined. Employment would decrease. The whole economy would falter.

Overlive politics concentrates on two targets. It dwells upon the tension and contention surrounding the quantitative division of the overlive production—the inequitable distribution of goods and services. This inequality is tied to the problem of race.

And it is concerned with the increasingly urgent need to accommodate somehow the impact of the technological achievement upon the ways things are regarded and traditionally done in this country. Automation reshapes job markets and redefines the idea and the role of work. Through the prolongation of the human life-span, medical science compels a reconsideration of the meaning of retirement from active production, and the relationship between work-for-money and the potential of leisure-time achievement. Communications and computer-recall capacities challenge the traditional right to privacy. The overlive technology subjects the established economic, sociological, and legal positions to hard new tests.

The unevenness of the technological developments stirs whirlpools of chaos which attract the overlive politician and greatly enliven the practice of his art. The politics of mass transportation is an example. The technology for producing cars and planes is more developed than the technology for the movement of cars or the control of airport and aerial traffic. The frustrations involved in getting from one place to another lead to an obsession with the problem of moving at the expense of the meaning of destinations. Having been somewhere is at least as significant as what happened while there. Travelers are converted into rushing tourist mobs, shooting snapshots frantically in order to produce some evidence that they have been somewhere and that something happened while they were there. The producers of vehicles and transportation services, in order to sell their products and services, persuade the consumers that motion is a virtue. Road building becomes a major source of pork-barreling even as the multiplication of vehicles chokes movement in the city and further pollutes the air over the places where the people live.

The alleged merits of motion in the overlive society extend to career goals, job opportunities, educational objectives, and creative experiences as well as to places.

The extraordinary success of the technology is the basis

for overlive optimism. The technology, exploding the old ideas of Time, Space, and Perception, clears the landscape for overlive renewal.

The supply of Time is increased by the extension of the human life-span and the conquest of space through instant communication and greatly accelerated transportation machinery. Not only are there additional life-years to fill, but within the bounds of these years, there is a new mobility for physical objects and for ideas.

The Time-Space breakthrough tremendously alters the opportunity for and the power of human perception. New breeds of machines (X rays, microscopes, satellites) live with men, directly extending the powers of their eyes, ears, and senses for feeling, moving, and thinking. The new mechanical sensory keys unlock the doors of the prison built around human genes by the special nature of our particular star.

The technology for perception is more advanced than the technology for increasing muscular power. Energy capacities lag behind capacities to perceive. Mountains can be moved. The moon can be visited. But eyes, ears, and minds now go through and over mountains and far beyond the moon. The power for perception dwarfs the power harnessed from the atom, and in the meaning of this imbalance is an explosive force greater than the bomb's.

As it reshapes Time, Space, and Perception, overlive's technology produces new knowledge at a rate much faster than it produces new houses, cars, B.S.'s or Ph.D.'s. Each penetration of time and space pours a steady new stream of data into the reservoir of knowledge. Just as the technology for the control of traffic lags behind that for producing vehicles, so the technology for receiving, containing, classifying, and recalling knowledge lags far behind our capacity to produce the knowledge. This gap affects adversely the ability of the scholars to interpret what is available to know. It produces a serious time lag between discovery and the application of what has been discovered.

No response to this floodtide of new knowledge seems possible except to grasp frantically at a small piece of specialization debris—not an ark, but a log; not a grand ship, but a slippery little raft. As went the dodo bird, so goes the Renaissance Man. In his place, tentatively, a new breed: the medical doctor, the college professor, the industrial manager—guilt-ridden and harried as he swims against the tide of the new knowledge in his specialty, so enervated by the upstream struggle to keep afloat that he is likely to be a conversational bore in any subject one inch off the dead center of his income-producing territory.

Overlive organizations and institutions are designed to contain and extend the technology's impact on Time, Space, and Perception. But their bureaucratic complexities, the codes of conduct they impose upon people, often limit the use of knowledge, blunt the edge of the intellect, and distort the expression of honest human feeling.

Bigness is a virtue among the organizations and institutions of overlive. There is an almost automatic translation of being the biggest into being the best. Being Number One, or at least Number Two and the Fastest Growing, is the common aspiration of profit-making businesses and nonprofit educational, technical, and cultural institutions. The coefficient of size is the centralization of decision-making power. Centralization implies a capacity for reaching decisions more efficiently and for the mobilization of superior intelligence in the decision-making process. The big corporation, the big hospital, the big university all arouse presumptions of durability, wisdom, and strength—the fate of the dinosaur notwithstanding.

The centralization of decision-making power is balanced by an emphasis upon the group or the team as the primary instrument for assembling information and shaping decisions. The group does more than bring together diverse bodies of knowledge and experience. It screens, selects, and interprets. It establishes the perimeters within which the decision must be made, and more often than not it makes the decision. Presumably the more who share in this process, the wiser the outcome. Responsibility for the decision is diffused through group decision making. The diffusion of responsibility reduces opportunities for subjectivity, privacy, and the expression of individual idiosyncrasies. Opportunities for individual privacy in thought or in action are circumscribed by the key position of the group or the team operating in the big organization.

Public opinion is a powerful force in the conduct of overlive affairs. Being accountable to the public is regarded as a special virtue. Much effort is spent by those in power in the attempt to control and dominate what the public thinks. The manipulation of what the public thinks eases the burden of being accountable to the public. Acting in public is often confused with or substituted for being accountable. Almost every overlive organization maintains a special office to manage its public relations, to express and interpret its actions to the public. The press release serves as a mediator between the responsibility of being accountable and the power of public opinion. The mediation is attempted with mirrors. The reality of the organization's intentions, policies, or actual conduct is reflected through specially created images. Image making becomes an art. The art consists of transforming reality into the images those in command think the public wants or will accept. When the reality departs from best estimates of what the public wants or will accept, the images projected depart from reality. To the extent that public opinion can be shaped and controlled by such images and reflections, monopoly, secrecy, and conspiracy may be concealed behind a pretense of public accountability.

The overlive organization encourages a division of labor between those who are supposed to think and decide, and those who are compelled to act as a consequence. Those who make the decisions are seldom in a position to implement them directly. It is not like art, where the painter paints. It is more like the college president's (backstopped by committees) deciding to construct a new building (with the approval of the board) which someone else designs, someone else contracts, leading someone else, finally, to dig a hole. He who is supposed to imagine the whole never gets his hands dirty digging the hole. He who digs the hole seldom can imagine the whole. In the composite contribution of the architects, the committees, the engineers, and the administrators, the project is depersonalized and departmentalized, and, more often than not, the achievement dehumanized.

Key decision-making teams or groups are mosaics of experts. Each expert asserts a presumption of monopoly in a vertical shaft of special knowledge. Each respects his colleagues' monopolies in exchange for their acceptance of what he reveals or chooses not to reveal—his selection of knowledge from his own monopolistic store. The non-revelation of monopolized knowledge is a powerful factor in maintaining the monopoly. The monopolization of special knowledge is essential to the self-esteem of the individuals who find themselves required to act, and especially to think, as members of a group or a team.

Organizations markedly different in purpose contain almost identical vertical shafts of specialized expert talent and activity. Large contemporaneous social themes, such as AUTOMATION, lead organizations opposed in interest— such as automobile companies and the United Automobile Workers—to compete for the same expert talent and advice. Expert services—legal, accounting, managerial, real estate, engineering, etc.—are in great demand among such diverse institutions as art museums, churches, and hospitals as well as among banks, manufacturing corporations, retail establishments, and agencies of government.

The top executives in the overlive society are interchangeable talent units. Retired university presidents move readily into the command of oil corporations or departments of government. Retired generals, admirals, or stock-exchange executives easily transfer to university presidencies. Those occupying these posts sit on each other's governing boards. They share clubs, modes of dress, common philanthropies, and political and recreational propensities. It is not uncommon for the top leaders of overlive organizations to remain ill-informed about the main subject matter of the organizations they lead. Their professed expertise is managerial— a claim to a familiarity with and a skill for the manipulation of power within the framework of the organization—any organization. In fact, survival in the retention of power often does depend more upon such a familiarity and skill than upon knowledge of the product the organization features.

The bureaucracies through which the overlive organizations exist favor institutional forms and operations over institutional purposes and the quality of production. This is especially true among service-producing organizations, like the educational, where ambiguity shrouds what "quality" is, and where it is difficult to measure "product" performance.

Teammanship and the expert use of knowledge monopolies are rewarded. Individualistic performances and a free trade of ideas are risky. The important thing is to look good. "Looking good" can be achieved through the placement of chrome on cars, or by the appearance of the wrappers or packages of products, or simply by the way college bulletins or recruitment brochures are designed and written.

This retreat from content helps the overlive organization acquire a personality of its own, one which is paramount to the personalities of the people it engages or serves. Soon things are done or not done For the Good of the Organization. Because the organization is larger than any one person in it, obviously The Good of the Organization is a larger good than the welfare of any one person or group of persons in it. The Good of the Organization is idiomatic in the language of overlive. The expression puts everything in its proper place—especially people.

The overlive organization generates its own Code for Survival, its own standards for successful individual conduct:

1. *Be Detached.*   The best human relationships are casual. Limit them to specific purposes, highly specialized subjects, and very precise problems.
2. *Be Loyal.*   Demonstrate fervent devotion and deep loyalty to the institution. In order to maintain the detached objectivity required to appreciate the institution's great mission, stay aloof from the realities of the lives of colleagues and avoid critical thought about the mission.
3. *Cultivate Insensitivity.*   Grow a thick skin. The show of emotion will almost always be taken as a sign of weakness unless the emotion is expressed in behalf of the official dogma—I'd Rather Fight Than Switch! Hail to Thee, Alma Mater!
4. *Vote with the Majority.*   Never, but never, dissent in the presence of a decision-making group. Dissent is often confused with disloyalty to the institution and its leadership. To show alertness and interest, occasionally question some facet of the system's detail. But beware a challenge to a basic tenet. It is better to be a part of an unwise course of action than to dissent, which is the unwisest act of all.

The economy, politics, and organization of the overlive society combine to form a very special response to the new technology's flow through the Time and Space dimensions.

The response is peculiarly American, but only because American conditions are the first to make overliving possible. These conditions frame some unique American problems. How can what overlive seems to compel Americans to do be reconciled with what they have always said and still say that they believe? Out of this question a clash of Goods arises—a contest among values which dominates the purposes of the educational system serving the overlive society. A New Way Challenges the Old Way, subverting even the language customarily used to describe or express the way we are supposed to be.

The Older Way:	*The Newer Way:*
Durability, frugality	Obsolescence, waste
Saving, pay as you go	Credit
The rugged individual	The group and the team
The property owner who runs his place	The manager who comes and goes
Conduct in the name of the person	Conduct in the name of the institution
Dispersal of decision-making power to the grass roots	Centralization of decision-making power
Staying put	Motion
Risk	Security

Schizophrenia is the unique overlive disease. The tension between the concepts in each of these columns has always existed, but overlive represents a subtle shift of emphasis and a sharp new confrontation. The shift embarrasses and complicates honest expression. A bridge of double-talk, suggestive of the Orwellian resolution of value conflicts, is thrown across the gap separating the way Americans used to think and still talk about themselves and the ways they now act. Even while the overlive man is standardized, domesticized, and socialized, he talks the language of individuality, competition, and free enterprise. Even while his real choices are aborted and his opportunities for self-governance reduced, he extols the virtues of democracy. This schizophrenia permeates the conduct and language of sex, family, religion, and politics in the overlive society.

The distance between what is practiced and what is preached especially appears to lengthen in the eyes of the young adult of college age. He hangs suspended between the professions of those whom he is supposed to respect and emulate—professions he suspects they no longer follow—and the uncertainties of an uncharted future. He may abhor the double-talk even while he masters it in order to survive. He seeks safety in the moment, which often makes him appear disrespectful of the past and disdainful of the future. The dances and sports he currently favors are furious distillations of action into droplets of time. They test and leave him spent in clean ways that, unfortunately, few other productive activities in the overlive situation afford. Far more than age separates him from those he is supposed to respect and follow—his parents, the clergyman, the president of the college, the chief officers of his government. And when all is said and done, the fact remains, if he is from the white, middle-class majority, he performs superbly well within the terms by which the overlive society measures acceptable performance. In spite of his occasional adolescent fits, he finally fits, and once he does, what is left for him to say?

The lower schools prepare the élite of overlive's youth to fit into the colleges and universities. The colleges and universities concentrate on the education of the young to fit into the overlive way of life. They are stations to prepare the most talented people for the next Great Leap forward into overlive future. As bureaucratic phenomena, they are beautifully designed to contain and perpetuate the meanings of the overlive system. They are perfect forms of the overlive organization, and only when viewed this way do they make sense.

Higher and higher levels of education are required to staff and maintain the overlive machinery. The time allocated for formal education is extended and filled with the old and the new knowledge, which is divided and subdivided into a proliferation of courses paced by the semester-hour credit system. The students then may be encouraged to shop and choose in the curriculum with some freedom, because those who have planned their "education" know that the choices, lecture-course packages, have little real meaning.

It is far more difficult to distill and teach the principles unifying a complicated field of knowledge than it is to define the field and present it in terms of bundles of facts. Fact bundles can more readily be reduced to survey texts, transported more easily through the lecture-hall distribution center, and policed more efficiently through the computer-processed examinations. And because of the plethora of facts in almost all fields, almost any selection from among them, especially if it fits the packaging system conveniently, is defensible. But the growth of knowledge in most fields subverts the durability, the staying power, the penetrating force of most such fact selections. Thus, within these terms, what is taught and the way it is taught are bound to create obsolescence. Such education is purposefully not meant to have lasting meaning.

Research is financed by and generally directed toward the service of overlive's power structure. The organization of research follows overlive organizational principles. Basic research, though often insulated from the direct influence of overlive political purposes, is quickly translated into the technology which serves those purposes.

The overlive university is especially proud of its educational service to the community. This service helps the overlive community hold itself together. It is poured like oil on troubled waters and, like oil, has the virtue of calming the surface while remaining separate and apart from the dirty realities of overlive politics, moral crises, and economic strife. Overlive universities make a big fuss about their neutrality and detachment in order to disguise their deep commitment to the future of overlive. They project the image of the community back onto itself, just as they receive and honor the community's reflections on their own mirrors.

The reception and processing of the talented young by the colleges and universities expose the two basic contradictions built into the overlive system. The system promises maximum freedom to all, but it rewards most those who conform best to its own standards and values. Accessibility to its benefits and rewards is promised to all, but by its standards and values the system precludes many. In a community where the people are least able or most unwilling to adhere to' overlive's standards and values, the system affords the least freedom. Access to the system's benefits and rewards is most limited in such a community. These contradictions are at the core of the black people's critique of what the United States has become. And that critique aims at the crux of the overlive dilemma.

The tension between black and white people permeates almost everything in our country. It upsets the performance of every basic institution in our society. It upsets our faith in the overlive success—in ourselves.

Racial strife has lengthened the distance between the ethics preached and the practice of religion in those churches organized under overlive principles. Denominational segregation in the South, the disintegration of middle-class congregations in the central cities, and the complexities (even the question of the propriety) of translating traditional religious thought into relevant social action have led to confusion and puzzlement among church leaders and managers. Many of the oldest and strongest churches have fled from the eye of the storm, retreating spiritually and physically to the perimeters of the problems.

Black is the primary color of the flow of population from the rural to the urban regions, from the Southern country-side to the cities, north and south. Blackness, together with the impact of the technology on the pattern of employment opportunities, colors the national manpower crisis. More and more of the jobs to be done require increasingly higher levels of educational preparation. Matching human resources to the demands of the economy makes the racist chapter in American history required reading for businessmen and educators as well as for the politicians.

The alliances traditionally holding the two major political parties together are unsettled by the insurgency of the black people. The recalcitrant membership policies of the labor unions, the continued influence of the Southern bloc, and the inheritance of political dominance in the great Northern cities where the conditions of poverty and discrimination are most explosive, magnify the tensions within the Democratic party. At a time when the conservation of old values and ways of acting seems inadequate or irrelevant, the Grand Old Party has yet to rise to the occasion, if it ever can. The militancy of the black youth and the growing suspicion against "white liberalism," make left and right, conservative and liberal, Democrat and Republican almost inapplicable terms. It is a time begging for political innovation.

But the federal context in which the two parties operate draws complicated boundaries around any innovative attempt. As population has congealed in the great urban centers, relationships between municipal and state governments and between Washington and the political territories where most of the people live, have become dangerously strained and ineffective. The magnitude of the country's problems invites an unprecedented concentration and use of public power. But at the same time, the very nature of the problems

calls for a revitalization of grass-roots democracy, the decentralization of public power in order to restore meaningful
connections between the people and the control of their own
destiny.

The proposal to decentralize the giant billion-dollar-per-
year, million-student public-school system in New York City
exposes many of the basic contradictions simultaneously.
The neighborhood school—the control of the school by the
community it immediately services—has long been a corner-
stone of universal public education in the United States.
But highly centralized, rigid educational bureaucracy in
New York City has failed to produce quality schools in the
black ghettos. Through more direct and greater community
control of their own schools, the black people hope to improve quickly the qualitative educational opportunities for
their children. Decentralization of the organization of the
schools accepts the fact of housing segregation as a reality—
at least for the present—in the educational environment.

Many who advocate decentralization in New York also
urge an early amalgamation of white suburban with black
central-city school districts. They argue that integration is
an imperative condition for quality education. What seems
politically and socially unattainable on the urban-housing
front, they aim to achieve through the reorganization of
educational systems. Making a distinction between the long-
and the short-range, a judgment about what is most urgent
and what should come first, may be difficult for the liberal
who links integration to the achievement of quality schools.
For the black parent, recipient of innumerable unfulfilled
promises, *not* making that distinction is unrealistic. The liberal may see integration as the surest road to quality, but
until he produces a political vehicle that will transport
people quickly down that road, his aspirations may seem—
at the very least—impractical to the black parent and, at
the worst, deceptions and sops.

Thus, the value-goal "integration" is set in opposition to the value-goal "quality education," and the going systems generate an expensive conflict between priorities at the very core of American tradition.

The American predicament is filled with such conflicts. Liberal and progressive politicians join the conservatives to acknowledge the practical impossibility or even the ideological undesirability of a monolithic, exclusively governmental solution to the immediate problems. They plead for a deeper commitment by private industry and commerce. Enlightened business leaders who really want to do what is right and are shaken by the growing violence in the streets where business is done, proclaim they want to help. But the old compass, the profit motive, somehow fails to guide the good intentions across the tricky currents of ghetto reality. Ghetto consumer potential cannot compete for the necessary investment capital. Mortgage profits are not large enough to attract the private housing developers. Insurance risks are too high. Confidence in the capacity for social change is too low.

Compromise, traditionally a great strength in our political conduct, searches for unique blends of the private and the public, the old values and the new situations. But the will to compromise is subverted by a history of too little, too late, too far off target.

Racism in America has a special quality for cutting through the fabric of our society, for pitting classes, life-styles, and life-goals against each other. Of course, the outrage of the poverty-stricken people in an affluent overlive society is directed toward the gross inequality in the distribution of material goods, in earning power and possessions. But the anger goes far beyond this now and precludes a simple material, economic answer to the nation's difficulty. The anger also strikes at the very meaning of possessing wealth on the majority's terms, at the conditions imposed by overlive upon the process of making a living, and upon

living. A connection has been made between the inequality
of economic condition and the meaning of the values upon
which the majority have apparently placed their chips. The
black people's critique of public education in the ghettos
also aims at the quality of white suburban educational
systems.

> Whites, and especially the white professionals, still determine
> our children's educational present and occupational future.
> We need not dwell upon the extent of the failures of this
> system. . . . Students must be involved in the development
> of relevant curricula reflecting the thrust of all Americans. . . .
> Students must be charged with the responsibility of the code
> of conduct in their school settings. . . . Students, particularly
> at the high-school level, like the rest of us . . . must have a
> right to make mistakes and grow from them.[3]

The black people's rebellion against political powerlessness
in the ghettos exposes the breakdown of political democracy
throughout the urban regions generally. Their indictment
of American life hits most painfully at the way the majority
lives. It touches upon the most sensitive nerves of middle-
class unhappiness and self-doubt. To questions about the
capability of the black minority, the indictment responds
with serious questions about the capability of the nonblack
majority. The basic issue has been transformed from black
to white to America. The issue is the capacity of the nation
to be what it has always claimed it is, but in fact has not
been.

The premises of American freedom and equality were
asserted long before the achievement of overlive success.
The premises did not anticipate the conditions which make
overliving possible. They were not especially designed to
accommodate and contain the consequences of overlive. The
overlive success presents a formidable challenge to the premises upon which American freedom and equality are based.

A powerful common denominator links the meaning of the
overlive success to the future of those premises. The thrust

of the technology, the uses to which the fantastic production is put, the future distributions of economic, political, and social power, the delineation of new values, and the new definition of quality in day-to-day life all presume and depend upon an extensively and uniquely educated citizenry.

This presumption and dependency may be dangerously unrealistic. It may not be possible to achieve the massive educational result required. Time is of the essence, and there may not be enough of it. Perhaps a substantial part of our people are simply ineducable, given the terms of survival the technology imposes. There may be no solutions to some of the critical problems overlive presents.

But no alternative is apparent. Education is the common denominator. The organization of systems to cope with and pass on to others the knowledge we already possess is central to maintaining the machinery we have already created. Education systems are the major variables with which we can work as we look ahead.

The institutions through which the highest levels of education are achieved occupy an especially sensitive and key position. Their influence reaches into the lower schools, shaping expectations, defining aspirations, and directing potentialities. They are the direct suppliers of the personnel without whose educated talents the military, industry, government, and the professions cannot function.

Far from being above and beyond the ferment and turmoil of power, America's colleges and universities are at the very center of the overlive predicament, at the very core of the American experiment. They are the embodiment of a new kind of institutional power in American life—perhaps the most strategic among them all.

My father just doesn't understand.

He admits that perhaps he and his generation have not made the system work as well as it should. But I

try to explain to him that's not the issue. The issue is
to change systems, to create a new one. He gets very
upset—emotional—or silent.

—From a conversation with a student at
Cornell University, February 1968

My son doesn't seem to understand.

His mother and I have made great sacrifices to pay
the bills at this university. We've not bought a car in
five years, and when tuition went up this year, we
washed out our trip to Florida.

And there are other things. His mother is not well and
when he brings home grades like this and talks about
taking off a year to hitchhike to the West, she gets very
upset—I mean physically sick. And then there's the war
and his draft status.

We only want him to have the things we haven't
had—the chances I never got. But he won't talk about
it. He just doesn't understand.

—From a conversation with a father at
Long Island University, February 1967

II

The University and
The Anti-City

In a luncheon address, Long Island University Trustee and Chairman of the Franklin National Bank, Arthur T. Roth, the man for whom the University's Graduate School of Business Administration is named, called on his fellow Long Island business leaders to join with him in a concerted effort to halt the "urban rot" which is spreading to Long Island. The urban rot, he said, "has already invaded our green island. Deterioration is right now undermining the health of our economy. Decay is costing us millions of dollars in lost real-estate values, lost taxes, higher social and welfare costs. If the rot spreads, the heavy pall of despair created by slums will drive out good business. The infection that destroyed New York City has spread to ourselves."

REPORT OF THE 1967 ECONOMIC
FORECAST CONFERENCE, HELD ON
LONG ISLAND UNIVERSITY'S MERRI-
WEATHER CAMPUS IN GREENVALE[4]

Take Harlem—Harlem's owned by whites and run by whites. We'll have Black Power when every cop in Harlem is black, every building and every business is owned by blacks, the schools are black, there's an all-black university, and the whole city of Harlem is run by blacks.

FLOYD MC KISSICK, FORMER DIRECTOR, CORE[5]

ANCIENT cities arose to protect the people. They were places for barter, trade, and defense in time of war. Modern cities are marketplaces for values and ideas, as well as for goods and services. They protect the people in the pursuit and enjoyment of the ways they have chosen to live, though during wars or internal rebellions cities may be the most likely places in which to die.

Industrialization, the handmaiden of the global growth of population, is an urban phenomenon. Economic and cultural progress will accelerate the rate of city growth—at least up to the point where population density frustrates all progress.* American cities are the test tubes in which the destiny of the American experiment is being shaped. People in other lands who aspire to achieve the best in an advanced American society may be overcome, if they succeed, by what is the worst in our cities.

Much of the criticism of the contemporary American urban scene is colored by nostalgia and mythology springing from the pioneer origins of the Republic. We tend to forget that life in the legendary log cabin, in the covered wagon, or in the New England village was often hostile to popular, modern conceptions of democracy, equality, cultural maturity, physical and mental health, and ease.

The nostalgia and myth represent a longing for simplicity. The urban environment is a direct consequence of human complexity. Complexity in environment stimulates and agitates those qualities in a species most critical to its survival. In the human species the mind is tested.

The natural thrust of the human mind is the introduction

---

* Earth population reached 250,000 two thousand years ago. It passed its first half billion at the time of the Pilgrims' landing on Plymouth Rock in 1620. The second half billion took another two hundred years. Earth population is now in excess of three billion, and the last half billion grew in eleven years.

of order into environment. Order cannot be equated with simplicity nor is chaos a natural function of complexity. Urban order is bound to be complex, more completely a product of human thought.

Thought, and its relationship to conduct, is what a university should be about. But most college spokesmen begin the definition of the institution of higher education by stating what it is not about. Invariably, they will say that a university is not just a library or bright new buildings or an attractive, tree-shaded campus. Almost any collegian, conditioned both to testing procedures and to the rhetoric of college presidents, can complete the sentence in twenty-five words or less: "A university is people who come together as a community of scholars to think" would be a satisfactory completion of the usual cliché.

"Coming together to think" is defined as noble. Taking the next step of·relating thought to action, while perhaps not ignoble, is not, according to the cliché, the business of a university. America's leading educational statesmen increasingly warn that our universities may lose their purity through excessive action at the expense of "scholarly reflection." Those with vested interests in the present Establishment rally around this banner with enthusiasm. Taking this position, therefore, has become almost the academic equivalent of the politician's glorification of Motherhood and the Flag. As the position becomes more popular and safe, it is, in the natural order of things, embraced by more educational leaders. The retreat to within the safe confines of the campus has been sounded lest the "mission" of the university be compromised.

The locations of most American university campuses are monuments to compromises, miscalculations, and expediency. Many are located where they are as a result of ancient estimates of where the people would be. Some, projecting the tradition of the monastery in the Middle Ages, were

planned to be where the people aren't—isolated in order
to provide the peace, quiet, and detachment the work of
the scholar allegedly requires. State legislatures dominated
by farmers more than a century ago put many of the great
Midwestern universities where they are—near the geopoliti-
cal centers of territories then agricultural—in places like
East Lansing, Urbana, Iowa City, or Columbus. Others
reflect philanthropic events like Long Island's suburban
C. W. Post College, which started in a manor house abandoned by the family whose name the college bears. Still
others, by accident or design, are in the great cities, located
on high-priced land, housed in converted warehouses, theaters, office towers, and brownstones, or in glistening new
steel and glass buildings which often cast shadows on nearby
slums.

Most of the country's outstanding universities are now
urban-based. Those which aren't are reaching out for the
nearest city as rapidly as they can: Illinois at Urbana for
Chicago; Michigan at Ann Arbor for Detroit; Wisconsin at
Madison for Milwaukee; Missouri at Columbus for St. Louis
and Kansas City, etc. The conditions which allowed many
of these institutions to become great, like Cornell in Ithaca,
for example, no longer exist.

Great cities naturally inspire great universities, and it will
become increasingly difficult for institutions of higher education to be great apart from the urban environment.

The flavor and style of national life, as well as its salient
issues, are urban. Three out of four Americans now live and
work in metropolitan settings. Less than nine percent earn
their livelihood in agricultural pursuits. Along the intricate
web of expressways and airlanes, through the instantaneous
flash of the television screen or explosion of radio sound, an
urban culture ties distant cities together and permeates the
remotest hamlet. The production of whole categories of key
national products and services is identified almost exclusively

with particular cities—clothes with New York; radio and television production and the publication of printed matter with New York, Los Angeles, and Chicago; the manufacture of steel with Gary and Pittsburgh; the production of automobiles with Detroit. Within each of these cities and industries a relatively small group of market men, designers, and production experts reach the grand decisions which influence the standards of taste, quality, and value Americans apply when they buy a new car, a new dress, a new book, or tune in a particular TV channel at a given moment in time. A relatively few are charged finally with feeling the national pulse and translating what they feel into a mass production which will influence the next series of pulsations.

The universities are also organized into such a network whose key lines are tied into a relatively few urban places. They are not and cannot afford to be detached from the sources of this urbiculture, from the origins of the action upon which the next thought steps so vitally depend.

While the impersonality of human relationships, the detachment from nature, and the frenetic tempo of daily routine may be the inevitable consequences of urban life, they are also the bench marks of the new national life, of which the university is an inevitable part.

There is an allure of simplicity in an administrative and technological approach to the huge, often vague, and always complicated issues of urban life. The sheer growth and new complexity of our academic organizations have evoked essentially administrative and technical responses. The leaders of the modern American university have reacted to their problems in the same manner as the political leaders· of our cities have to theirs. But their reactions have not bridged the growing schism between the academic administrators and those who teach, or stemmed the tide of student unrest. The assault upon the problems of health, slums, congestion, and corruption requires the most effective mobilization of technology and administrative innovation. But monumental convention arenas and schemes for amalgamations of governmental agencies do not make a city any more than the computer processing of admission papers, the mere manipulation of credit-hour systems, and victorious basketball teams make a university.

Renewal, housing, traffic, police, crime, air and water pollution, food and shelter for the poor, and the provision of public education—these are the problems that preempt the day-to-day operations of municipal governments, capture headlines, and imprint what "city" is all about upon the popular understanding.

These problems suggest what a city is, how it may be defined. The basic terms of reference are physical, material, and economic:

land occupied and the uses made thereof;

the size and density of population;

the number and character of enclosed spaces and the pattern of their arrangement relative to pedestrian and vehicular thoroughfares;

and the other service and economic aspects of group life, especially those subject to statistical analysis and quantification.

Still, these qualities do not by themselves account for differences in the quality and tone of public and private life in various, large, densely populated areas—areas which because of the population concentration exhibit all of the problems mentioned above. Des Moines, Denver, Kansas City, Dallas, and Los Angeles have tempos and personalities distinctly different from those of San Francisco, New York, Atlanta, Chicago, and Boston.

Suburban rings around Los Angeles, Chicago, and New York contain populations almost as large as the cities they encircle, and within those rings there are pockets of density as great or greater than the averages for the cities to which they relate. Yet these rings clearly are not citified territories.

Detroit, with its two million people plus two million more in its metropolitan region, is an especially interesting place about which to ask: Is this a city?

Detroit occupies a large land area even relative to its large population. The majority of its people live in single-family dwellings. Green grass and trees are plentiful within the city; high-rise residential developments are not. One can ride for miles through the city into suburbia without noting any significant change in the land- or city-scape. The central commercial section of the city is as desolate and deserted after dark as a suburban residential street. Commerce and retail business have been divided into thirds among the older downtown center and two vast shopping plazas imposed on the borderlines of the suburbs at the outer extremities of the city. There are few good restaurants, and these are dispersed. In fact, there are few places in the city which invite public discourse, leisure activity, or conversation. There is a civic center and a cultural center, and within each there are superb facilities often used by first-rate organizations. Detroit has an art museum and a symphony orchestra worthy of any great city. But the neighborhoods containing the excellent galleries and halls which accommodate these and related kinds of institutions are relatively empty of inviting places to go to or to walk in, before and after events.

Perhaps the most striking feature of Detroit is the power monoliths which hold it up as an entity. It is a city of power unities—almost of monopolies. One bank is much larger than the others. One department store virtually dominates that category. There is one major industry. There is one art museum, one orchestra of repute, one industry to which a large share of the rest relates, and one union which is organized around that industry. There is one large public university and one large Catholic university. In this setting, the utility monopolies—gas, electricity, and telephone—are at home. Indeed, it can almost be said that decisions on any subject vital to the welfare of Detroit—the development of the port, cultural life, race riots, or the economy—can be made at a conference attended by a top officer from one or two of the automobile companies, an executive of the U.A.W., one officer each from the big department store, the big bank, and one or two of the utilities, one university president, a newspaper or television executive or two, and a few well-known patrons (or matrons) of civic causes (who most likely will be connected to people in the other categories represented at the conference).

It is not the mere presence of slums, pollution, and corruption (and the presence or absence of high-priority programs for their eradication or control) which distinguishes a city from a non-city. The land surface occupied and the density of population are relevant but not conclusive "city" indices. What counts are the configurations of these elements *plus* other conditions which produce certain attitudes and styles among the leaders and those led, conditions which influence attitudes toward these problems and the parameters for decision making.

Foremost among these conditions are the opportunities for mobility, for the movement of people, ideas, and things— movement from place to place and from status to status, social, cultural, and economic; mobility in coming to possess and to use power—all kinds of power including political.

Mobility presumes the risks of moving and a certain attitude toward taking those risks, a certain receptivity toward the idea of moving up or down or laterally. The willingness to take risks is something for which Americans traditionally take pride in themselves. Risk taking is associated with adventure, with pioneering. The emphasis given to its deterrents and preventives in our individual affairs and in our corporate life is one of the sophistications of the overlive epoch.

The generator of mobility is the presence of a large variety of alternatives—the ever-present imperative to choose.

"City" as a way of life implies the potentiality and the necessity for recurrent choice in almost everything—jobs, housing, amusements and leisure pursuits, modes of dress, architecture. Only a large variety of truly different and contending alternatives gives meaning to the act of choosing—variety in the marketplaces, the economy, the arts, politics, and associates and friends.

Different people, when free to choose and provided with some real alternatives, naturally choose different things. Choice from among a large variety of alternatives in any category produces differences of opinion and a constant contention for power. Conflict and controversy are implicit in "city." City people have a different receptivity for and outlook toward conflict. They develop a different threshold of tolerance for it. Politicians in every country in the world must take this fact into account as they bargain for urban, as distinguished from rural, support.

The very essence of "city" is the promise of a redistribution of power. The point of the mobility, choice, and ongoing conflict is the opportunity to change the distribution of power. The dynamics of "city" is the ongoing process of power redistribution. Understanding this process, one can see why most suburbs and many places we identify as cities through the criteria of size and population are in fact non-cities. They are status-bound as well as status-conscious places. Detroit is one example.

The contemporary urban ghetto is anti-city.

The ghetto is a static island in the sea of urban change. In it, segregation by race and economic status precludes variety, an abundance of alternatives, and effective choice. There is no place to go within the ghetto. The chances for getting out are slim. There is no mobility. But there is "hustle" and conflict.

"Hustle" is survival action—the exploitation of the exploited by the exploited. In the modern ghetto, hustling is motivated by something more than the keen sense of frustration felt by the more aggressive and cunning individuals. It thrives because of the powerlessness of an entire community, and a community-wide recognition and defeatist acceptance of exploitation as a way of life.

Conflict within the ghetto is a direct function of the more basic struggle between the ghetto and the rest of the city. The inequality of this struggle subverts the quality and meaning of controversy within the ghetto. The ghetto's internal conflicts are generated by an inadequate and meaningless supply of alternatives. They proceed from a premise of immobility. Even as the powerless compete for inadequate power supplies, they suspect that nothing will really change. The competitions become factional feuds, generating even greater disorder. They have the effect of perpetuating the inequality of the contest between the ghetto and the rest of the city. They squander limited powers.

Poverty programs, social-welfare efforts, and university uplift projects have generally failed in the ghettos because they have not been addressed effectively to the powerlessness of the communities. Most of these efforts have viewed power merely as a quantity rather than as a process. They assume that an increase in the supply of food, housing, clothing, educational facilities, and other welfare services will achieve a fundamental alteration of the pattern of exploitation dominating an entire community.

This approach fails because the quantum of power injected is never enough to create anything like a parity between the standard of life in the ghetto and that in the rest of the city. The quantities are just enough to excite and intensify the internal competition among the powerless. They are never large enough to enable the powerless to change the condition of their community.

The approach fails also because it assumes that the powerless can never really alter the condition of their own community. Not only are the power packages brought into the ghetto too small, but the power in them is prepackaged. The decisions about what goes into the packages are made outside the ghetto. This has the effect of underscoring the proposition that the rich, the powerful, and the beneficiaries of overlive education understand the reality of being poor better than the poor. If the ghetto happens to be black or Puerto Rican or Mexican, this approach states an ethnic-racial conclusion. Power becomes white. Its importation under these conditions has the effect of agitating the feeling of exploitation and inferiority.

Jacques Cousteau concludes his brilliant documentary film on the life of sharks with a sequence showing a brave diver on the floor of the sea holding out bait in his hand to attract the sharks. At first, a few come and nibble cautiously at the bait. They become bolder and more aggressive, and then more come. Then more, until scores of sharks are dashing and slashing at the bait. Of course, the bait is not enough to feed them all, and soon there is a frenzied competition in which the sharks wildly strike at each other, at anything which moves or crosses the path between them and the bait. The turmoil is vicious. The diver is hastily drawn up to the surface to escape the deadly, primitive chaos.

More often than not the inducements dropped into the ghetto disturb whatever pattern and balance of community life is there, and whip the local leadership and the people into a frustrating competition destructive of what unity power they possess. (Perhaps that's the purpose of the bait in the ghetto.) But for the American commitment there is no escape from the frightful adventure beneath the surface of the ghetto sea. No mother ship floats on the surface of American life with equipment for pulling the commitment up from the danger zone. The victims threaten to bite the hand that baits them, to destroy the force that tempts them but does not satisfy them—even at the expense of self-destruction.

Conflict within the ghetto usually terminates in the disengagement of the ghetto people—a popular disinclination to participate—or in street violence, crime, and riot, which may be viewed as the only alternatives available to express the longing for mobility and the chance for change, for a redistribution of power.

American universities claim to be, and in fact generally are, going communities. Many of them are consummate welfare-state communities, feeding and housing the student citizens (and often the faculties, too), regulating their political relationships, providing medicare programs of their own, and maintaining, in addition to the parking lots and athletic stadia, systems for influencing and shaping the cultural and social lives of their people.

The more detached and isolated a university campus is from the city, the greater is its need to construct and maintain the total paraphernalia of a going community. The people have to be fed and housed, and given aspirin when they have colds. If the people are young and away from home, assumptions are made that they have to be taken care of in a lot of other ways too. Moreover, they have to be taken care of in a manner to which they are more or less accustomed. Or so it is assumed.

But even in the great cities the concept of "campus" as a separate, distinct, and more or less self-contained community persists. It is a community beyond the classrooms; its borders are the curbstones on the city streets surrounding the place, and the jurisdiction of its special body of laws regulating sex, food, residence, cars, liquor, clothes, political activity and expression extend right to the curbs—and sometimes beyond.

Within these communities, rank and status are fixed. The citizenry is divided into four basic categories for the purpose of government—students, faculty, administration, and "others." Within these categories, the students are pegged by year of entry, the faculties are ranked and given tenure, and political power is apportioned among administrators in accordance with rigid bureaucratic hierarchies. Salary rewards and tuition assessments are related directly to the status structure. Rates of annual salary increments are established according to the ranks. Tuition fees vary according to undergraduate, graduate, or professional-school status. Curricula are measured and paced in keeping with the credit-hour degree system. The entire campus is wrapped in the principle of separateness and detachment—a principle designed to impress upon those subject to it an appreciation for their differentness, and upon the public beyond a respect for the alleged objectivity, neutrality, and élite quality of the academic "community."

Within the urban campus what meaningful alternatives do the university's citizens enjoy? To what extent are they encouraged to participate in choice that counts? Of what does mobility consist in the academic community? What is the threshold of tolerance for controversy and conflict on the campus? How may those who teach and those who are taught achieve the reordering of their own affairs in pursuit of their own best interests?

The salient qualities of the city—the opportunity for mobility, the abundance of meaningful choices, the respectability of and tolerance for controversy—are imperative to the pursuit of university goals. The freedom so essential to the higher learning cannot exist under ghetto conditions.

Most of our urban campuses have become ghettoized; they are anti-city. They have become hostile to the idea of city—to the life-style the qualities of city impart.

As it confronts the turmoil and the variety remaining in the city, the university (as an institution) is often inept and ill-equipped. Too frequently the assumption is made that the university can simultaneously be neutral, catalytic, and intellectual—that water, oil, and fire can mix. A catalyst is by its nature not neutral. It is a force which releases energy in

a particular direction. The leaders of an urban university—
which by its location, if nothing else, has a vested interest in
the life of the city—possess the power to affect the public
destiny. A university in the city, just by being, affects that
destiny.

The University of Illinois persuades the public power in
Chicago to uproot the residents of a slum on the West Side
and to finance the new Circle Campus. Columbia, unable to
pack up and move operations to the safety of Westchester or
Long Island, acquires more properties in and about Harlem
and hires its football players, armed with clubs, to police
them. Clark Kerr and Ronald Reagan meet, and the consequences are something more than a friendly conversation
about California weather.

Universities are social institutions and forces, whatever
else they are. As Sir Eric Ashby puts it, "Universities do not
exist simply for their own sakes, as daffodils and sparrows
and mice do; they have a purpose."[6]

By the assertion of their ambitions and purposes, universities declare a position and, having done so, they invite a
popular inquiry into the tradition of neutrality to which they
may like to retreat when the going gets rough. The people
dislodged on the West Side of Chicago claim a vested interest, and they want to know what the Circle Campus means
for them.

President James Perkins of Cornell University says, "It is
legitimate for a university engineer to design a bridge,
but not to involve the university in building it."[7]

But all may see from the window of an airplane on the
approach to Ithaca that Cornell has helped to build Ithaca,
has imposed upon that town an architecture and a design for
community·life from which the students and the townspeople
may not escape. In fact, the University has become involved,
had to become involved. Simply by being itself, by pursuing
its self-interest, it has not only designed a bridge and built

one, but also created the *necessity* for a bridge between itself and what it has done to the community.

No longer can the academic leaders and the research professors avoid direct conversation with the people in the places where the universities are. Given multimillion-dollar budgets, extensive real-estate holdings, and future property needs, pretensions about and real connections to the national purposes and welfare, the universities must confront changing views about their institutional responsibilities. Older notions about scholarly detachment and academic neutrality are shields which will be pierced by those who understand the institution's vested political and economic interests. The campus, especially the campus in the city, is no longer a safe retreat.

The idea of "campus" is archaic in the modern urban setting.* The wide-open spaces, the monumental and inflexible architecture, and the insulation to which it aspires combine into an anti-urban phenomenon.

The campus is more than a place and a way of arranging physical resources. It is a system, and is meant to be a way of life. It assumes the turning inward of the flow of human relationships. Its success depends upon imposing an isolated, contrived community upon the lives of its inhabitants. It is tenured, by the ranks, on a full-time basis in a world which requires taking risks and discouraging the security of mediocrity, in a time when rank is not enough, and in a society whose goals preclude the full-time devotion of a man's energy to any one pursuit—which requires that every citizen engage on many fronts simultaneously.

Neither the lives of those who teach and learn, nor the problems confronting them, nor the configuration of urban talents conform to the campus version of life. "Campus" organizes the university's outrageous presumption that it can

* In the Latin language the source of the word "campus" means a flat place, a field, or an open plain.

and does monopolize the best talents in order to do what it claims to do. In the great cities this presumption is absurd.

The hard problems of urban life (and thus of contemporary American life) do not conform to the ways universities are organized. In general, universities are organized according to the academic disciplines. The hard problems of urban life disregard these classifications. They transcend them.

These problems no longer revolve simply around training men to earn livelihoods (universities have mastered this kind of production problem reasonably well), or even upon updating professionals once exposed to higher education (a responsibility in which the universities still have a long way to go). The hard problems arise in the realm of each citizen's public connections to his fellows, in the areas of public policy making, cultural quality, and men's relationships to the state and, beyond buying and selling, to each other.

A list of the hard problems must include the mass media, the life of the aged, juvenile delinquency, the popularization of the arts, the condition of the black people in America, the conduct of our nation on the international front, peace. Each of these issues comes to focus in urban arenas, for no one of them can be approached without the mobilization of the talents and power uniquely present in the cities. Almost always the most urgent and interesting urban issues are controversial, and the really significant ones are those which draw men out of their occupational slots into the public forums, where their conduct will be governed by knowledge and experience mainly unrelated to the know-how they possess as wage earners.

The universities in the city are often not the best and never the exclusive reservoirs of recorded modern knowledge. In most cities, the public and nonacademic technical libraries are more extensive and accessible compendiums of knowledge than the universities. Many urban art museums possess both scholars and treasures far superior to those possessed by the universities. Practicing politicians sometimes display far greater wisdom and teaching talent than practicing political scientists. Throughout American urban society, many institutions other than the universities provide laboratories and workshops for some of the nation's keenest minds. They compete for the same talent the university often claims to want.

This competition underscores a challenge to the university as a thriving and healthy center for thought, and suggests strongly that our universities, often being inefficiently organized bastions of conservatism, are not always the friendliest settings for thoughtful men. Indeed, throughout U.S. institutions of higher education, the most critical and controversial men are almost always critical first of the academic institution and are at war almost always with the traditional parts of the university itself. They are compelled to do battle in the defense of the exercise of their talents, in order to be themselves. Their alternative is to abdicate the responsibilities of citizenship in the university community.

The pretensions of the university lead to tremendous waste in the current processes used to plan and build academic facilities. This waste is directly reflected in the cost of education and is one of the two largest components of the expense. Many of the new buildings, created to endure a half century or more, embody imperfect translations of what is needed to house the *present* educational operation. Surprisingly few faculties and administrations convey clearly to architects and engineers what they are doing *now*. There is an almost complete failure by those responsible for building universities to anticipate physical needs ten years ahead —let alone fifty.

For the city-based university, the circumstances of the urban environment and the rapidly changing nature of the content and methods of education raise the questions: Can the academics anticipate their own future needs? If not, should the institutions be built to endure forever? Instead of the conventional approach to building academic facilities for permanence and endurance, why not new standards to honor *impermanence* and to accommodate honestly the reality of change?

Almost no collegiate facility should be financed or built to endure for more than a decade in its original form. The educational enterprise should be housed in "tents"—the best coverings and enclosure of spaces an advanced technology can produce, "tents" which can quickly be put up or taken down, moved or altered to suit the consequences of the incredible knowledge growth we already confront.

Monumentality contradicts the terms of contemporary learning. It is a social waste and a major deterrent to learning progress—an academic luxury. Sometimes monuments are important to the human enterprise. They may exalt, beautify, inspire awe and respect for authority and tradition, or illustrate aspirations and purpose. An educational place may do all of these things *if* education happens in that place. If an occasional monument is desired and can be afforded on the university's place, fine. But in the setting of the city, a monumental university is an anachronism. In time, even pyramids are reduced to grains of sand if the systems which created them have outlived their purposes, and die. Pyramids were built to contain the dead and to honor them. A university's view of the past and the present should be different.

The overlive economy and technology promote urbanization—the concentration of people in the places where the jobs and the opportunities are. In our overlive society the low-achievers, the poor, the rejects—especially in the great urban centers upon which the progress of the economy and the technology depends—may be identified mainly by color and race.

Class status (the life-styles made possible by varying levels of educational and economic attainment) combines with racism to create residential and recreational ghettos circumscribed not only by wealth but also by color, religious affiliation and ethnic background. Styles of life vary among these ghettos, but life within each is marked by homogeneity.

In some respects, for some purposes, people live and work in these urban ghettos voluntarily, by choice and preference. In other respects they are imprisoned in these ghettos against their will. The popular push for the "integration" of American society often fails to allow for the subtle distinction between voluntary and involuntary segregation, for the healthy tension between the thrust for social equality and the respectability of being different. The problems of class in this country are intricately interwoven with a uniquely American racial theme.

Against the backdrop of this racial theme, the economic and technological forces of overlive tend to produce *anti-city* patterns of life and ways of thinking even among the great concentrations of people comprising the growing urban regions. In the cause of our most enlightened traditions, these forces often promote uniformity and homogenization (integration?) in some sectors of the society even while imposing involuntary segregation in others. The alternatives framed—involuntary homogeneity or involuntary segregation—are hostile to the idea of a city. In many ways the overlive economy works for the concentration of people in an atmosphere hostile to the idea of city life.

The technology has been employed with great success to achieve the dispersal of light manufacturing (furniture, food processing, etc.), the assembly of heavy manufactured goods (automobiles), certain kinds of highly technical industries (electronics, drugs), and commerce (banking, retailing). But its success has been far more limited in key kinds of endeavor which are the main wellsprings of *city* culture.

For the purposes of day-to-day top-level managerial decision making and master processing, industry relies heavily upon the concentration of talent, often under one roof in a single office tower, and the location of this concentration close to similar ones housing the leadership of other industries, often on the same street. The dispersal of manufacturing and assembling activities in the automobile industry, for example, has been matched by the continued concentration of executive talent in office towers in a relatively few cities— mainly New York, Detroit, and Los Angeles. Within a population region, banks with scores of branches located in suburbs and far-flung neighborhoods maintain central towers to house leadership proximate to other banking headquarters, stock exchanges, the brokerage and related industries. Most clothing is now manufactured in the South, but many of the industry's key decisions are made in New York.

Notwithstanding advances in the art of packaging and in the technology for transportation and communications, no one has yet quite discovered how to "disperse" great museums of art, great orchestras, or great centers of the dance or theater. In some science endeavors, the variety of talents required compels the location of the institutional home in a city center where the talents, and the resources needed to sustain their work, are available on call. Closed-circuit television and intricate radio and telephonic networks have yet to replicate the vital processes which occur when scholars and students actually associate together.

Dispersal within population regions has been most successful where the organization and use of physical energies are emphasized, and least successful where the organization and use of intellectual and artistic powers are concerned. The former pursuits are subject to standardization; they can be duplicated on a mass basis. The latter cannot. The former can be carried forward at some distance from the strategic activities of different endeavors. The latter require proximity and association. The products of the former can be transported without direct injury to the human soul. Often the movement of the "products" of the latter is one of the most difficult steps in the production.

Intellectual and artistic work does not favor dispersal. But the life-style of the middle class does favor the dispersal of the residences made possible by the fruits of that work. The decentralization of commerce in material goods and services catering to the physical needs of life follows the dispersal of middle-class residences. The result is a pattern of culture-rich, slum-ridden cities and comfortable, middle-class suburbs stricken by a culture poverty. The two parts are tenuously linked by an insufficient transportation network, a communications technology controlled by the lowest common, middle-class denominators, and a political system volatile with great new internal contradictions.

Superimposed upon city and suburban neighborhoods alike is a system of lower education embodying and projecting the dominant, middle-class values of American society. The system favors the success of the children of that class. It defines achievement and excellence in terms of a white majority's experiences, needs, and sense of values. It works against success by outsiders, by those whose experiences are different. The system operates to exclude the outsiders it has helped to create even while standing for the principle that they ought to be included.

To the outsiders the alternatives are frustrating and confusing. Some want "in," and their anger is a straightforward reaction to being kept out. They may drop out of the schools, but they are certainly not yet dropouts from the American promise.

Others despair of ever getting in, and this despair takes the form of rejecting the system. The system theoretically invites integration; in practice it segregates. It is possible that the main thrust of Black Power and Student Power is not the rejection of the system, but the unveiling of its pretensions, the calling of its bluffs. But the advocates of the New Powers are not sure, and as it licks its wounds, neither is the system.

What a city must be may not be compatible with the ideas

the majority of the Americans seem to be accepting about how they want to live, or overlive. The majority is using its great power to insulate itself from the significant American failures. In its pursuit of the American rewards, it has moved away from the meaning of the American promise. As the problems within the cities mount, the majority grows more and more concerned about the conservation of what it already has. It moves away from the problems in order to defend itself better.

The campus in the city, as a system, as a model for community life, too often becomes a vehicle for carrying anti-city and even anti-learning values into the educational situation.

It promotes a very refined classification and segregation of people and pursuits according to standards which are no longer relevant. It encourages the separation of the commuting students from those who are resident—of those citizens who by circumstance (and often by choice) move freely in the city from those who are encouraged to remain detached. It imposes, or at least it works hard to impose, a social and community life suburban in tone and quality, innocuous, bland, and perfumed.

The laws of the campus are expressed negatively. They are aimed at *prohibiting* the citizens from succumbing to the evil temptations of city life. They seldom state what the people can do, but they elaborately spell out what is *verboten* regarding the consumption of liquor, sex relationships, political activity, etc.

Dormitory life is unnatural. Society between the sexes is purposefully staged in settings open and public and necessarily stilted. At best, a good dormitory is a high-class barracks—an arrangement of living patterns closely akin to the housing of low-rank military personnel or suburban housing projects, but lacking some of the niceties and safety valves of either.

Association between student and teacher is discouraged in almost all campus places except the classrooms. In the classrooms the association is usually meant to be formal and even remote. The students and the teachers eat in different places. Student eating places are generally expensive, and the quality of the fare is indefensible. In fact, in most city settings, the cost of university housing and food exceeds the expense for comparable facilities and services off campus, and the quality and style of both are generally inferior on campus.

The style of campus life works against intellectual or social intercourse among people of different ages. The young are herded with the young—the older, with the old. The grouping of faculty offices by the disciplines and the disciplines by the colleges discourages communication among people pursuing different interests within the faculties. In the faculty dining rooms there are science tables and history tables, and discourse between historians and chemists is restricted to perfunctory greetings as each moves to the tables where their colleagues are. The students and the teachers use different bathrooms and have access to different resources in the libraries. And, of course, in many places the administrators are apart from and above it all.

The style of city life and the changing content of knowledge combine to suggest that the insulation of "campus" will no longer do in the city setting. A new approach to the identification and engagement of talent is imperative, and this approach requires new ways of accommodating the talent once it is recruited.

Many of the people upon whom the university will have to rely should not and will not devote their full time to the institution on its present terms—isolation, exclusivity, detachment. Our universities must begin to mobilize the best of the total community talents in order to teach, do research, and serve society. The part-time academic connection should become more prevalent than the full-time affiliation, especially in the city where the competition for brain power is bound to intensify.

The university in the city—reliant upon a large variety of industrial, governmental, and artistic resources and talents, but unable in view of the competition to monopolize the best of these talents available—will be compelled to redefine the meaning of "campus." Necessity leads to an extension of the day-to-day operations beyond the pieces of real estate upon which the institution's special buildings stand. The function of the university inevitably must move into the theaters, museums, industrial laboratories, libraries, and centers of financial, social, and political research housed in other urban institutions.

The emerging "campus," therefore, will be coincident with the pattern of location of central urban resources and reach out to where those resources actually are.

Great museums may become the future "departments of art." Symphonic and musical organizations may become the future "departments of music." Research centers in banking and finance may become the foundations of future "departments of finance and economics." Government commissions and research staffs may become the backbones of future "departments of political science." Basic elements of the city itself may compose the format of the future university—the new higher-learning enterprise. Finally, the city itself may become the new campus, and learning may become intricately interwoven with and addressed to the day-to-day activities of the people.

The new approach to the city's talents and its nonacademic treasuries of art, knowledge, and wisdom implies a redistribution of power within the university and between it and the city. Relationships among university people and between them and others are bound to change, and the change is bound to put a fresh light on the connections between thought and action. This is the crucial connection—

constituting a new kind of knowledge—the linkage between the habit of thinking and the necessity for acting. The meaning of the quantity and the content of this new knowledge, and its impact upon the society we are building, turn upon how the educational organizations achieve this connection.

The student demonstrations in Germany have stirred up deep emotions here, and have highlighted the essentially undemocratic structure of higher education in Germany. Many of the reforms now being considered here were stimulated by the radical student groups. The students are demanding parity in every decision-making body of the university. They believe that the university must stop being an ivory-tower in our country—that it must become integrated into our society.

—Excerpt from a letter from a young German faculty member of a distinguished university in the Federal Republic, March 1968

The German students are on collision course with the academic and governmental administrations as well as with the academic and social hierarchies.

It is no accident that the student rebellion began and had its highest escalation in the greatest cities of our country—in Hamburg, Berlin, and Munich.

—Excerpt from a letter from a German graduate student at Universität Hamburg, December 1967

III

Power and the University

Education is thought about and as it is thought about it is being done. It is being done in the way it is thought about, which is not true of almost anything. Almost anything is not done in the way it is thought about but education is. It is done in the way it is thought about and that is the reason so much of it is done in New England and Switzerland. There is an extraordinary amount of it done in New England and Switzerland.

In New England they have done it they do it they will do it and they do it in every way in which education can be thought about.

I find education everywhere and in New England it is everywhere, it is thought about everywhere in America everywhere but only in New England is it done as much as it is thought about. And that is saying a very great deal. They do it so much in New England that they even do it more than it is thought about.

GERTRUDE STEIN[8]

THE ANCESTOR of the American university arose on another planet, the planet medieval—now dead.

That planet did not orbit around a science sun. No sphere circled it casting a maddening lunar light, unsettling the minds of the people with wild ideas about governing themselves. Status and order were its guiding stars. Everybody clearly had a boss—on the job, in the church, in the realm.

Most did not have to think about honoring their mothers and fathers. Circumstances and blood were enough.

Sir Eric Ashby writes that

> the institution has preserved its identity of pattern not only in time but also in space. . . . This survival of identity is a sign that the university has adapted itself to successive cultural environments. . . . What has survived and is significant is the social purpose of the university, its independence from Church and State, and its peculiar method of internal government.[9]

But survival has not been easy for the university. Edward H. Levi, president of the University of Chicago, notes that the institution has always had a problem just enduring. "The university and its friends struggled greatly for its existence." Mr. Levi adds:

> The fact there is an unmet need does not at all mean that a university is best equipped to take it on. Even if it is, the added function may place such a burden upon an institution as to defeat its basic purpose. . . . The freedom of the university and its scholars to refuse to take on new assignments is extremely important.[10]

The price of institutional endurance must be measured in terms of the balance between what the university refuses to take on and what it decides to do. The meaning of its freedom, its capacity to be free, can be identified only in the total pattern of its positive and its negative choices. There are risks pursuant to both kinds of choices.

Throughout its evolution the university has certainly adapted itself to "successive cultural environments." There is ample evidence of its powers of adaptation even in our own time. Hitler may come and go, but Munich and Heidelberg go on forever. The British Empire may fall, the island's brains may be drained, but there'll always be an Oxford. Industrialization, technology, and psychiatry may penetrate the curriculum of Harvard, but the penetration has had little discernible influence on the structure of the internal government of that university or any other.

There is the other side of the coin: the assignments a university decides to take on and the bases for such decisions— the kinds of students it decides to admit; the places at which it decides to build and the style it adopts for building; the government contracts it seeks and accepts; the balance it achieves between research and other pursuits, between liberal arts and technical, undergraduate and graduate; the new centers and institutes it establishes; the kinds of faculty and board members it values and recruits. At the core of the problem of what a university should *not* do is a series of very basic questions about what it should do. How may a learning institution best be organized to express its commitment to reason, to pursue its search for basic knowledge, and to select and honor those cultural values which deserve continuity and preservation? The leaders of our universities ought to approach these questions with candor and without undue prejudice against an American society whose aspirations are quite different from those of any other in which the university has endured.

In the defense of its integrity, an American university's search for basic knowledge may compel its programs, its administrators, its teachers and students to go onto the streets. Sometimes the best sources of knowledge, the raw materials for scholarly work, and the minimal actions required to maintain a society in which a free university may exist, force the institution to confront the unmet needs, to take on the new assignments. Sometimes such needs and assignments are irrevocably connected, not only morally but also intellectually, to the university's search and mission—its very reasons for being.

The policy and action lines between academic ideals and academic realities are extremely tenuous indeed in a sophisticated technological society, almost every dimension of which critically depends upon the superior mobilization of intelligence. The lines would be tenuous in such a society even if it did not aspire to the American freedom principles. When an urban ghetto encroaches upon a campus, or when an expanding campus encroaches upon the living communities around it, whatever the university decides or doesn't decide has the effect of reshaping its traditions and its values and purposes. In a country where public health services are a primary political concern, in an era of organ transplants and a growing capacity to control genetic arrangements, both scholarly and ethical problems link the life-science pursuits of the university—its practical, day-to-day research and teaching operations—to the decisions being made in the society all around it. In fact, whatever its intentions, the university actively participates in making decisions which have impact far beyond itself.

Should the institution take a position regarding those policies which guide a government in the recruitment of young men for the military? Should it undertake research in and teach others about the nuclear and space-science fields knowing how intimately related these subjects are to national security? Monetary policy? Executive leadership in business? The problems of municipal government? The education of nurses, lawyers, or the administrators of action programs in the ghettos? Food production? How is the institution to decide where to put its chips? Where is the basic knowledge? Through the study of what is the commitment to reason best honored? What is academically "pure" and what is not? Whatever the traditional language used to describe lofty academic purposes, the practical pursuit of these purposes has taken the university down the tortuous road of political, economic, social, and cultural decision making.

Evolution does not mean the same thing now it once meant—for mankind or for the institutions men create. The

raw forces of nature count for less. The raw problems arising out of man-made environments and cultures count far
more. This fact of evolutionary life means that all of our
institutions, in order to survive, must more actively engage
in the flow of events around them. Detachment may be as
dangerous as commitment, even for universities, for which
freedom is the essence of being. The defense of freedom now,
more often than not, depends upon intelligent participation.
No longer can the freedom of the university be defended
best from behind stout, greystone, ivy-covered walls. Perhaps
the most effective universities must now be built without
walls. Perhaps the maximum freedom to learn is best
achieved by tearing down the barriers closing the realm of
the university off from the arenas of worldly action.

When some semblance of organized learning fled from the
closed world of the medieval monasteries of Europe, it took
to the streets of the cities—first in Bologna and Paris, and
later in Cambridge, Salamanca, and elsewhere. The flight
was an initial but necessary step in the secularization of organized education, in the long struggle to free formal learning from the domination of particular religious and/or political patrons.

The cities were the natural breeding places for the freedom movement. A city attracted students through the mag-
netic pull of great teachers who dwelt there. And where else,
reasonably, were the scholars to dwell? As Lewis Mumford
points out, the main thrusts of organized learning—"cultural
storage, dissemination and interchange, and creative addition"—are also "the three most essential functions of the
city." The ideas of "city" and "university" share common
grounds.

The original makers of the freedom movement—students
and master teachers—were shaped into coherent groups by
the pressures of practical problems whose solutions required,
or seemed to, the organization of power bases and the use of

power. Early in the twelfth century many students were drawn to Bologna. They came from all over Italy and from many places throughout Europe. Charles Homer Haskins describes the conditions which they faced upon their arrival in the city, conditions which brought them together to form a powerful lobby.

> Far from home and undefended, they united for mutual protection and assistance, and this organization of foreign . . . students was the beginning of the university. In this union they seem to have followed the example of the guilds already common in Italian cities. Indeed, the word "university" means originally such a group or corporation in general, and only in time did it come to be limited to the guilds of masters and students. . . . Historically, the word "university" has no connection with the universe or the universality of learning; it denotes only the totality of a group, whether barbers, carpenters, or students did not matter. The students of Bologna organized such a university first as a means of protection against the townspeople, for the price of rooms and necessaries rose rapidly with the crowd of new tenants and consumers, and the individual student was helpless against such profiteering. United, the students could bring the town to terms by the threat of departure as a body, secession, for the university, having no buildings, was free to move, and there are many historic examples of such migrations. . . .
>
> Victorious over the townsmen, the students turned on "their other enemies, the professors." Here the threat was a collective boycott, and as the masters lived at first wholly from the fees of their pupils, this threat was equally effective. The professor was put under bond to live up to a minute set of regulations which guaranteed his students the worth of the money paid by each.[11]

What unfolds is a story whose main line is the reciprocity of power. Under the circumstances given, the professors organized to protect themselves.

Excluded from the "universities" of students, the professors
also formed a guild or "college," requiring for admission
thereto certain qualifications which were ascertained by
examination, so that no student could enter save by the
guild's consent. And, inasmuch as ability to teach a subject
is a good test of knowing it, the student came to seek the
professor's license as a certification of attainment, regardless
of his future career. This certificate, the license to teach . . . ,
thus became the earliest form of academic degree. . . . And
the ambitious student sought the degree and gave an inau-
gural lecture, even when he expressly disclaimed all intention
of continuing in the teaching profession.[12]

This exchange between the teacher and the taught was
straightforward and direct, uncluttered by the intervention
of managerial middlemen, unsullied by the authority of a
board of trustees. The students wanted to learn. They needed
access to the men of learning. They valued the mark of a
"learned man", membership in a particular guild. The professors, on the other hand, were committed to a calling, and
they wanted to get paid. These ingredients made for relatively simple transactions.

Dr. Haskins asked, "What . . . is our inheritance from the
oldest universities?" The answer, he suggested, was not

in buildings or a type of architecture . . . in academic form
and ceremony. . . .* It is . . . in institutions that the university
tradition is most direct. First, the very name university, as
an association of masters and scholars leading the common
life of learning . . . the notion of a curriculum of study,
definitely laid down as regards time and subjects, tested by
an examination and leading to a degree . . . the faculties . . .
with their deans, and the higher offices such as chancellors
and rectors. . . . The essentials of university organization

---

* Lewis Mumford writes: "In the original layout of the colleges in Oxford
and Cambridge, mediaeval planning made its most original contributions to
civic design: the superblock and the urban precinct divorced from the
ancient network of alleys and streets."[14]

are clear and unmistakable, and they have been handed down in unbroken continuity. They have lasted more than seven hundred years—what form of government has lasted so long?[13]

But what has lasted? What is the relevance now of the part of the inheritance that has endured?

The conditions of overlive have transformed the association between masters and scholars. The quality and content of the curricula have been utterly changed by the new knowledge. Between Bologna and the university serving the overlive society lies something vaster than seven or eight centuries. In its trip from Bologna to modern America, the university has experienced the rise and fall of Student Power, the rise and fall of Faculty Power, the rise and decline of the powers of the Church and the State over the university, the ascent and steady deterioration of private philanthropy and the authority of the governing board, and now the sway (and often the swagger) of the academic managers, the technicians, and the overlive efficiency experts.

What remains are calcified organizational forms—empty shells of dead guilds inhabited now by the new middle-class bureaucrats. What remains is the name "university", the idea of curriculum—often refined and specialized to a point of disorder and irrelevance—and the titles of office describing the hierarchy which has gained the power to rule, even if it is unsure of the meaning of having the power and often is embarrassed by the responsibility of having it. What remains is the façade of the tradition, the pretense of other-worldliness, the guise of neutrality. Behind all this is an institution transformed by the possession of a tremendous new power, a power made possible and deeply influenced by the circumstances and the conditions of overlive.

A complicated corporate structure has been built to house the new power. The language of overlive dominates the description of the corporation. The overbearing uniformity and standardization of the system (credits, grades, courses, ranks, tenure, degrees, departments, etc.) are presented in terms of increasingly irrelevant diversities (the alleged significance of being large or small, public or private, "liberal" or specialized). Crucial authoritarian powers (to admit or to exclude, to grant or withhold the degree, to "educate") are justified in the name of promoting the free enterprise of talent and ideas and equality of opportunity. A twentieth-century jargon has been invented to describe the educational corporation and how it works—a technical language especially designed to enhance the corporate mystique and to remind the public of the limits upon its ability to understand. The institutional stories are told in bulletins opaque with obscurities, labyrinths of legalisms, scores of pages explaining how people may get through something while giving only the vaguest hint about what it is they are going to get through.

Course titles are grouped authoritatively under departmental headings as if the mere listing lends credibility to the sequences and the subject matter the titles vaguely suggest.

The credit-hour currency is purposefully complex—two hours for this and three hours for that, distributed symmetrically over categories called "majors" and "minors," "required" and "elective," but always adding up in a magically standardized period of time to a required total which can be exchanged for one of an assortment of degrees. The credit points not only measure the work cost of the reward, but also the dollar price. The credit-point currency units can be negotiated in academic "banks" across the land, providing the local "bank" has been certified as "safe" by some regional agency of the national accrediting reserve system. The constitution of the reserve system is still another subject. The regional agencies are artful organizations whose movements are as intricate as whooping-crane dances.

Those who teach are listed by the ranks and by the degrees, and how a teacher is judged for promotion from one rank to another is a subject the academics are loath to discuss even among themselves. The possession of degrees is usually accepted as conclusive evidence of excellence. "Ph.D." means "able scholar, teacher, and gentleman." One standard routinely used by the accrediting agencies to certify solvency is to add up the number of Ph.D.'s, department by department, engaged by the petitioning academic bank. But just as in the Law of Monopoly it is not clear what percent of a market a producer must dominate before he is put in the prohibited category, so it is not certain what percentage of an academic bank's staff must wear the Ph.D. button before the institution is put in the "safe" cubbyhole.

The process of deciding who will be kept out of the university is called "admissions." It is based upon the administration of batteries of tests which few members of the administrations or faculties have ever seen, taken, or understand. Those who give and "grade" these tests seldom teach and rarely participate in the policy decisions affecting what is taught. The tests are backstopped by elaborate application forms and sometimes by personal interviews. At many places the tests, the forms, and the interviews are all superimposed upon a political process which depends upon who knows whom. Many institutions, especially the younger ones, apply two kinds of admissions standards—a cosmetic one, pasted on the public face of the institution through its official declarations; and a private one, through which all of the official criteria are breached until classroom seats and dormitory spaces are filled sufficiently to make the annual operating budget tenable. In the established "prestige" schools, where the demand for entry exceeds the supply of places, rigid admissions criteria guard the portals—tests couched in a language and based upon a cultural know-how often irrelevant to the large new classes wanting in and led by society to believe that they should get in. The admissions process is pregnant with value judgments about the educational quality of the lower schools, the talents and potential of humans, and the pretensions and intentions of the admitting institution. If anyone ever came to understand the real meaning of these judgments, he would understand a great deal indeed about higher education.

"Grades" are a system through which academic failure or success is measured. Only simple literacy is required to know the difference between an *A* and an *F*, an 82 or a 91. Official "transcripts"—bank statements of credit-hour and learning deposits and withdrawals—are issued periodically and contain simplified explanations of the accounting code employed. Like bank statements, they are produced by IBM machines.

But it would take a Solomon to understand the bases for the variety of grading systems used by different universities or even by departments within one institution. It can be rather unpleasant and awkward to certify that a human being is a "failure"—even in a single course. The faculty member who fails too many, however, runs the risk of being identified as a failure as a teacher by the system to which he belongs. There is a limit to how many enforced "dropouts" an institutional budget can endure. Too many failures also cast a bad reflection upon the admissions process employed. In transferring currency units from one bank to another, credits "earned" vie with grades "achieved" in importance, at least within the broad range of "Excellent" to "Mediocre" (as distinguished from "Mediocre" to "Failure"). Finally, the degree is the great leveler. The fact of its possession comes to eclipse the importance of what happened along the way. For the job market, and for most other purposes, the degree is honest. It is a frank indicia of an "educated man," conclusive of the irrelevance of a *C* average, a *C—* or a *B+* composite. Grades are an embarrassing subject which faculty members generally avoid discussing with each other. From the student's point of view, obviously the important thing is to understand the game and to play it so that one survives.

All of these mysterious devices and systems, and more, are the symbols proudly displayed to insure a popular respect for the formidability of "university." They are among the formal underpinnings of a complicated, institutionalized, professional enterprise. They go far to establish the principle, or at least the illusion, that no human being can really learn unless he "goes to college."

The cost of going to college has risen spectacularly, especially since World War II. This phenomenon is often explained in the public-relations style of an electric-utility monopoly, whose prices constantly rise, but whose full-page advertisements and TV commercials repeatedly remind us that when we flick on a 6o-watt bulb we're really getting more for our money—even if we have to pay a little extra for being reminded.

Of course, the price of everything has gone up since World War II. The two biggest cost factors in higher education are the cost of the buildings and facilities in them, and the cost of the human talent required to staff the enterprise.

Construction costs generally have risen, and the machinery used for science education is especially expensive. But a special premium is paid to honor the assumptions of the academic managers regarding what it is appropriate to build, and how. The adoption of medieval and rural academic architectural traditions in the modern urban setting has not only helped to inflate the cost of academic construction, but has also led to some strange artistic and functional results.

The value put on specialized human talents has also risen, and the competition for such talents has intensified. But a premium is paid here, too, in order to implement the academic prejudices about what talent should be engaged and how it should be employed. The nine-month academic calendar, notions about the virtues of reduced teaching loads, the tenure system, and a resistance to the realities of the urban talent pool all contribute to the budgetary pressures on this front.

The private sector of the education industry is virtually pricing itself out of the market, or, to give its managers the benefit of substantial doubts, is being priced out by circumstances beyond its control. The Carnegie Corporation has initiated an extensive study of this crisis in the education economy under the direction of Clark Kerr, the former President of the University of California. On the public front, education is now generally the largest item in the budgets of municipalities and states (followed by welfare), and in Washington no departmental bureaucracy and budget have had a more extraordinary expansion than Health, Education and Welfare (with the possible exception of Defense).

Bigness in America often carries with it an implication of superior efficiency. A big university will presumably not only be more efficient than a smaller one, but, partly because of the greater efficiency, it is supposed by many to be qualitatively better as well.

The giant public systems are committed to growing larger. Bigness has brought with it unique problems of control and management which seem to threaten realization of the efficiency gains that being big is supposed to bring. The purse strings of public higher education are usually held by politically conservative state legislatures. These political agencies are bedazzled by master organizational schemes, centralizations of educational administrative power on statewide scales in order to "coordinate programs," and to "reduce overlap, duplication of effort, and interinstitutional competition." To lead one of these public systems or institutions, a man must have a reputation combining political conservatism or, at most, middle-of-the-roadism, with a capacity for the skillful, businesslike management of increasingly rigid versions of state socialism. He must be able to bridge the gap between what the conservative politicians preach and the practices they inspire in behalf of maximum educational efficiency. Monopoly is honored in higher education these days as the "efficient way," and merger is as prevalent in this sector of American life as it is in most others.

The tuition and boarding costs of going to college have gone from an average of $900 per year to something more than $2,400 between 1947–48 and 1967–68 in the private schools, and from an average of something less than $600 to more than $1,200 in the public institutions during the same period.[15]

For the typical American family the cost of an undergraduate degree is far in excess of its annual food bill, the expense of purchasing and maintaining two automobiles, or the downpayment on a mortgage for a middle-class three-bedroom house. Parents are deeply concerned about the expense of what they buy. But in this part of the economy there are practically no reliable consumer guides to help them. Once they make a commitment to a particular college they have less recourse, should the services delivered prove inadequate or faulty, than a ten-dollar customer at Macy's. This is one part of the American economy where the principle of *caveat emptor* operates unabated. Disagreement between tuition-paying parents and educational institutions invariably centers on what's happening to the child of the former in the care of the latter. Confrontations on the occasion of such disagreements almost always proceed from the presumption of mistake or misdeed by the consumer. It is almost inconceivable that the institution, wrapped in the impersonality of its "standards" and evaluation and counseling "systems," could be wrong. In no part of the American economy does the complaining customer begin with so many strikes against him. And in few parts of the economy are the alternatives so bleak. The "fact" of a customer's failure is made part of an official record—a transcript which is honored or given great weight by producers everywhere in the industry. Uncooperative customers are in effect blackballed.

The annual working budgets of the colleges and universities are privileged documents. There is virtually no accountability to those who pay the bills among the private schools. Even in the public sector notions of academic independence circumscribe and delimit accountability. Expenditures under federal grants must be accounted for after a fashion; periodic reports are given to foundations, presumably telling them how their grants are spent. But those who pay tuition—which even among the economically "strongest" schools still accounts for one-third to one-half of annual income—receive no reports or accounting except for the vague public-relations statements sometimes printed in fund-raising brochures.

It is considered very bad form to think or talk about the relationship of students and their parents to colleges and universities in terms of buyers and sellers of strategic services. Words like "industry" and "customer," when applied to education, are thought to be degrading and damaging to the rich conceptual tapestry hung between those who operate the institutions and the publics they serve. This tapestry is meant to conceal the configurations of power within the educational corporations, and the direct bearing the use of that power has upon the vital interests of those served. When there are no "customers" and there is no profit-making objective, corporate management is freed from its most threatening restraints.

Few boards of trustees, few faculties, and few state legislatures or regulatory bodies understand the multimillion-dollar operating budgets of the educational institutions for which they are nominally responsible. To the extent that the flow and deployment of these substantial sums are understood by anybody, the academic administrators and managers have the edge. And it is doubtful how far their understanding extends to the impact of expenditure upon the quality of output. Treasurers and accountants can arm a university president with what he needs to make a budget presentation to his board of trustees. But these fiscal officers are usually ill-equipped to make value judgments about educational policy, and so are the boards. A great deal depends upon the leader's outlook in the climate of the pressures to which he happens to be subjected at the moment.

Not too long ago, the presidents of three private universities in the East—located near each other and appealing essentially to the same potential students—met secretly at lunch to contemplate tuition policy for the coming fiscal period. Each was charging between $42 and $46 per credit point. They decided simultaneously to raise tuition in each institution to $50 per point, which subsequently they did. Had they been the chief executives of oil companies or dairies, their conduct may have amounted to illegal conspiracy. But in the field of education what they did was but another routine example of thoughtful fiscal planning and interinstitutional cooperation.

About one aspect of the economic power of the educational institutions the public can be sure. No sum of money appropriated in support of the educational enterprise will ever be "enough." No university president will ever tell his alumni, students, and benefactors that the institution has "enough." The public can expect little help from the professional educators in the definition of what "enough" is or ever will be. It is doubtful that the professionals know or, if they did, that they would tell. Never having enough is one of the dynamic conditions for the survival of our colleges and universities in their present forms. It is a great source of their social and political powers.

The powerful and strategic role the university now plays in our society and the elaborate corporate devices invented to express that role, predetermine the outcome, almost prejudge the resolution of the issue about its identity, its purposes. By accepting the power and seeking more, by maintaining the devices and elaborating them even further, the institution guarantees for itself an identity crisis, a grand confusion of purposes. No wrapping of medieval concept and tradition can successfully contain the remarkable new content of the academic package. Such a wrapping is bound to rip, to tear, and to embarrass him who tries to carry it from one place to another. It complicates and deters delivery.

Lewis Mumford comments:

> As the Church ceased to be the repository of new values, the university gradually took over some of this office. This fact placed a premium upon the detached pursuit of truth, as the dominating life-value, and has ignored in large degree the realms of esthetics and morals. Thus the university has become a classic example of that overspecialization and limitation of function which now curbs human development and threatens even human survival.[16]

"Overspecialization" is an irrevocable and imperative co-efficient of civilization forces far larger than any our universities may counteract. In fact, overspecialization is not something which the academics fear or deplore. Quite the opposite: they welcome it and build upon it. It is the main generator of faculty self-esteem. It is the main basis for the securing of operational power by the academic managers. To become overspecialized is the principal motivation of the students. The widely accepted and well understood value of overspecialization is one of the important common denominators of the modern university community.

It is *over*diversification and *over*participation in the solution of the salient problems of our time which the academics see as a real and present danger to the endurance of the traditions some claim they cherish. Fears about the future of the university in America

> boil down to two primary concerns. The first has to do with the external relations of the university—that it may lose its identity. The second has to do with the internal cohesion

of the university—that it may lose its capacity to manage its own affairs.[17]

There is the fear that the powers that flow from being overspecialized may be eroded by engagement with issues and problems which elude specialized answers. There is the fear that, through the further commitment of the university's powers in controversial areas which affect the very maintenance of those powers, those in command may lose control. There is the fear that those who venture now beyond the neatly redeveloped superblock campuses into the alleys and streets of the cities may get hurt. And, indeed, they may. Unhappily, the alternative is bleak. A failure to venture may be even more damaging. The leaders of higher education are now beginning to learn what leaders of lower educational systems in the great cities have been learning the hard way since World War II. Educational leadership is a very high-risk calling, the maintenance and exercise of which involves living dangerously.

Recently the trustees of the Carnegie Foundation for the Advancement of Teaching issued a summary of their discussion of "The University at the Service of Society." They said:

> There are, theoretically, two diametrically opposed positions which the university may adopt as it considers its public-service role.
>
> In the first of these, public service is regarded as an inappropriate and irrelevant function for the university on the grounds that it is inconsistent with an academic institution's basic responsibilities for teaching and the discovery of new knowledge . . . that it is the duty of university leaders not to be engaged in selling the university's services but in protecting its essential integrity. . . . The university in this view should abjure any conception of itself as an activist shaper of the larger society. . . .
>
> At the opposite pole is the view that, among all institutions in the nation, the university has the greatest responsibility

to be a shaper of the society. . . . It must be engaged, activist, reformist . . . prepared to reach out into the larger
community.[18]

Naturally, the trustees at Carnegie reject the two extremes
and argue for a "practical middle ground . . . a more realistic
stance." But the problem here is not an abstract choice between two conceptual extremes—"Let's protect integrity"
versus "Let's shape society." The problem is the reality of
university power—what men and institutions will do to get
it, defend it, and use it. The problem is the source of the
power and its connection to survival.

In its power to admit or not admit, to expel those admitted
or to reward them with a degree, the university influences
directly the future earning power, the class status, and, more
immediately, the time and/or necessity of military service
of those who seek its services. Few institutions in American
life can wrap so many elements of powerful influence into
one package. Solutions to the most cutting problems of our
time—race discord, poverty, national security and peace—
hinge on the completest engagement of technical knowledge
and intellectual talent. The university advertises itself as the
primary source of such knowledge and talent. Even if this
advertisement is misleading, the university is a most aggressive and powerful competitor against all other such
claimants.

Notwithstanding its reliance upon the European academic
traditions, the American university has staked out a unique
claim to fame, mainly because the aspirations of American
society are unique—or have been. The goals of higher education in this country have come to combine Horace Mann's
conception of education as a magic key opening the door
to economic equality with Thomas Jefferson's conviction that,
among a self-governing people, education insures the application of some reason to the conduct of the affairs of state.

Our universities are expected to be the doorways to the popular aristocracy through which every man may go from anonymity in the lower ranks to the highest rewards this society promises.

The relationship between our educational institutions and the society which supports them is dramatically different. The key to that relationship is not how to keep people out in order to maintain an old standard of values. Instead, it is how to get people in, given the people with whom we must work, and what "in" means, given the aspirations of this society.

Consequently, the relationship of the educational institutions to the other great configurations of organized power in the country—to the churches and the state, to the professions, and to industry and the military—is transformed, if not quite completely reversed. In the past, the university's struggle for independence from external strategic power centers, "independence from Church and State," was a dominant theme. But now the university itself *is* a strategic power center in American life—a power partner in the management and direction of the whole, without whose close collaboration the other centers cannot proceed far.

From the medieval beginnings of the university right through its nineteenth- and early twentieth-century versions in the United States, the preparation of an élite to lead was stressed as one of its primary functions. At first, the performance of that function took the form of conveying what was known in a relatively few basic categories of knowledge. Later, it came to include the encouragement and accommodation of new discovery, the addition to the store of knowledge through research. Throughout, the relationship of the university to the majority of the people was indirect and remote, through the educated élite, through the chosen few who were expected to lead as custodians of the religious inheritance, as lawgivers, as healers, as protectors and patrons of the civilized graces, and as teachers of lawgivers, theologians, healers and aristocrats.

But now the university operates on and directly serves not only those who will lead, but also those who may be led. The filters between its production and the popular mind are extremely transparent. The osmosis between its values and mass style, opinion, and value is almost as immediate as the capacities of the communications technology. The centrality of the academic power station in the landscape of national life—the intimacy of the connections between it and the other major power stations of the society—underscores in a new way the power of knowledge, the power that comes from the control of its production as well as of its use.

The American university exerts a new kind of institutional power, a power flowing from its possession of extensive properties and huge material wealth, from its capacity to withhold or to give strategic services, from its willingness or reluctance to respond to the pressures and problems besetting the other primary power centers, from the quality and character of its responses. It leads because of what it does or does not do in the classroom and beyond it. But it also leads actively in the vital arenas far beyond the classroom and its own campus. It leads in its own name, a fact of life about which it still feels some embarrassment.

In the Foreword to his "multiversity" book, Clark Kerr writes:

> The basic reality, for the university, is the widespread recognition that new knowledge is the most important factor in economic and social growth. We are just now perceiving that the university's invisible product, knowledge, may be the most powerful single element in our culture, affecting the rise and fall of professions and even of social classes, of regions and even of nations.[19]

We may well ask about the university—its traditions, its organizational forms, its pretensions and prejudices: What form of government has lasted so long? Perhaps it has lasted too dangerously long. The old ideas must be reexamined, the old habits, perhaps, cast off. Traditional notions about scholarly detachment, the meaning of "objectivity," the necessity for a disconnection between academic thought and social action, old ideas about how the human learns, the retreat from the streets of the city into the superblock campuses, the ways talent may or should be organized and used—all of these and more deserve an intensive, fresh look.

Finally, the price of being powerful, against the backdrop of what education is supposed to be all about, must be faced —and probably paid. The university can no longer avoid the risks of taking positions on the conduct and goals of those with whom it has chosen to wheel and deal. Indeed, it has no choice about this. So long as it chooses to wheel and deal in the maintenance and extension of its own power, it takes risks—whether it consciously supports and approves the status quo or not.

The twilight of an older academic era cannot be conjured away. The sun has set. No critique of the American university can go far in the absence of a confrontation with the society in which the academic institution is a power partner. The university, like the new America it serves, is compelled to move along toward the dawn of something new.

———————

I'm still teaching economics in Algiers. There are about ten thousand French people teaching in this country. The system of education here is a transplant from France. Most of the programs don't fit Algeria. Most of them are out of date in France.

There are some students in the University who resent the imposition of the French educational system here, and the misuse of power it represents. They want to do something, but they don't know what, and they rarely move beyond the protest stage.

My own job is frustrating. I try to think. I speak much. I talk to many people, but I cannot act. I cannot take any decision. I do not have responsibility for what happens. I am an outsider.

—Excerpt from a letter from a French graduate student teaching at the University in Algiers, December 1967

IV

Thinking in an Action World

> It is existence and reality that we wish to comprehend . . . and when we strip this statement of its mystical elements we mean that we are seeking for the simplest possible system of thought which will bind together the observed facts.
>
> ALBERT EINSTEIN[20]

Every university claims to create a "climate for learning." A climate for learning is part of the institutional sales pitch, like a winning football team or a program for a year's study abroad. *The* climate for learning is a Caribbean isle in January—halcyon, undisturbed by strong winds, warm and sunlit, a shirt-sleeve (or at most a tweed-jacket) climate conducive to leisurely contemplation in shaded groves or secluded campus alcoves. In the climate for learning the students and teachers decide virtually nothing. They just think.

If places with such climates ever existed, few do now. Campus climates are more like the rapidly moving eyes of hurricanes, intermittent calms surrounded on all sides by terrible, swirling storms—wars (and protest demonstrations to stop them); plagues (and federal grants to wipe them out); slums (and institutional schemes to keep out of them).

Industries, governments, and almost every other configuration of community power are forever demanding that the
scholars think in their behalf or, worse, *act* in support of
their purposes. Along the cutting edges of these demands
and expectations the line between town and gown is drawn
—a border between the sanctity of institutionalized thought
and community action.

An invitation to act is often viewed by the teacher-scholar
as a real and present danger to his main business. His main
business has something to do with thinking.

But he is human. He does exist, and in one way or another
the reality of action is a problem for him, too. His claim to
special knowledge, as a professional man, attracts invitations.
He may think he prefers to stand aloof, to teach, write, do
research, and "think." But the enticing invitations are there.
He can't help himself. He, like the institution for which he
works, gets involved.

"Getting involved" is one of the origins of the schism between those who manage and those who teach in the university. Administrators are always issuing invitations to act.
Presumably they possess the power to act. It's a part of their
lore that faculties invariably resist action. Faculties claim
they are disinterested or powerless in the realms over which
the academic managers preside. There is a gentleman's
agreement of sorts to maintain an uneasy peace. Generally
the administrators concede the curriculum to the faculty in
return for almost everything else. But a clash of positions
divides the academic house when some detail of existence
and reality arises, like next year's salary schedule, a shortage
of parking spaces in the faculty lot, or a proposal to adjust
the allocation of credit hours among the various disciplines
represented in a degree program.

The adverse academic presumptions about action operate
with a special clarity in the case of the student. By the definition of his status, the student is a junior-grade thinker. He

has so much to learn about thinking that action is especially deleterious to his progress. In a nutshell, "the student is a student. He is at the university to learn, not to manage; to reflect, not to decide; to observe, not to coerce."[21]

On this front the administrators and the faculties are likely to agree. But not the students. About the content of their own lives (including the learning experience), many students expect to manage, do decide, and, learning from, reflecting upon, and observing the examples provided by the administrators and the faculties, are prepared to use coercion when necessary. The others all do. The academic system invites them to, in spite of its admonitions to the contrary.

Academic prejudices about the relationship of thought to action in a learning enterprise are deeply embedded in the content of curricula and the methods used to teach. These prejudices go far to encourage class warfare on the campus and to increase the tensions between the campus and the rest of the world.

The object of thought is the discovery of some order in the chaos and uncertainty of our existence. Thought is an exploration of infinite variety and continuous change in a search for the enduring, the unifying, the universal. Thinking is a part of reality. The consequences of what we think are real enough.

Being human we have a choice of different platforms from which we may launch our thoughts. We have the capacity of perspective and, within limits, of choice. We can ignore the universe some superhuman force made. Godlike, we create our own. There are some New Yorkers, for example, whose universe is limited essentially to a place of residence, a place of work, and a long, dark, dirty, and noisy subway tunnel connecting the two. They go under the foundations of the city's great treasuries of art and culture, beneath the ferment and variety of its political and social life, and they undermine the meaning of the city for themselves. Some such New Yorkers are college students, and still others are their teachers. There are millions of urban Americans for whom life is a long, dark, dirty, and noisy tunnel connecting dreary, dull, inane destinations. What these people think may not influence the course of public events, or even their own lives. But within these limitations, they do think. If nothing else, they sometimes think about being in the tunnel and enslaved by the destinations.

Thought may soar high on its trip toward the enduring, the unifying, and the universal, but it begins from the humble soil of "the facts." Facts result from human observation. Between this observation and the upper reaches of thought is an elaborate structure for classifying knowledge, for arranging the facts in some order, for establishing relationships among them and between groupings of them, and for recalling and using them. Most learning organizations are attempts to institutionalize this structure, and to implement or assist the process it implies.

A large library is an example of how facts and ideas are classified. Universities are organized in terms of the basic classifications. Programs of study are developed out of the organization and in conformity with it. Academic politics result from the conduct of groupings of scholars within the structure of classified knowledge, and the operation of an administrative hierarchy geared to the classifications.

Facts spawn facts. The proliferation of them is one of the most significant phenomena of our time. An extraordinary technology has erupted from the facts. Each new discovery sets the stage for subsequent ones. A new light-year built into a telescope adds volumes to our libraries and may add a whole new sequence of courses to some university's curriculum. The sheer quantity of knowledge places an almost unendurable stress upon our mechanisms for classifying, absorbing, and organizing what is known.

The expansion of the content of each knowledge classification has a profound effect on the conduct of scholars and, through them, on the institutions in which they work. As each knowledge territory grows larger, the mind is enticed deeper into it. At the same time the range of classifications to which any one man may apply his thinking powers is narrowed. In medicine, law, and most professions the general practitioner gives way to the specialist. Disciplines of all-encompassing content, like philosophy and theology, are subverted by this process. They end up jargonized and irrelevant and, in the academic power systems, pushed off into dark corners. Philosophers end up talking to each other and virtually to no one else. Not only is the dialogue between the scientist and the humanist impaired, but the conversation between the physicist and the chemist becomes difficult and often impossible.

While the quantity of knowledge is overwhelming, the rate at which its content changes has tremendously accelerated. Radiation belts flow into the stream of our consciousness with the suddenness of a satellite's orbit. Electrons become waves *and* particles, subverting the classical law guiding the nineteenth-century physicist that something must be either *A* or not *A*.

So great is the growth of fact and so far-reaching and rapid is the rate at which the meaning and content of the facts change that a serious question arises about what a fact is. For the educator who professes to "teach the facts," the prior question arises: "What are they?" Planning an educational bill of fare—a curriculum, a degree program—is converted into a delicate and difficult art of selection. What is important, and what is less important? Is anything more important than anything else? How does one tell what is important? Is the mere durability or endurance of an idea decisive? Is the number of people who believe it crucial? Is the standard of utility—the usefulness of the idea—paramount? As the educational selection process approaches the frontiers of knowledge or the borderlines of ignorance, the controversial issues dominate. Consequently, the curricula of the "free universities" which the students have started in reaction to the established institutions are dominated by such subjects as the Vietnam war and Black Power. And within the universities ideas about which least is known, the scary ideas such as "Slum," "War," and the "Meaning of the Technology," are broken down into disparate parts and hidden away in the corners of the traditional classifications such as Sociology, Economics, and Engineering.[22]

As observation increases and more facts and ideas accumulate, new syntheses unfold and old ones collapse. Systems of thought and mechanisms for classifying creak and wobble as they strain to accommodate the accretions and changes. New classifications are created to house new lines of thought, as in the case of cybernetics. Old classifications combine and fuse into new forms such as biophysics or geopolitics. The going power system within the university, the prevailing pattern for the allocation of credit hours—the number given within a four-year degree program to each classification— are upset. New arrangements threaten the status and prestige of the old. The science sector expands; literature contracts. The demands of the proponents of graduate and professional education become more strident; the capacity of the advocates of the undergraduate to resist recedes. Chaos overtakes the schools of teacher education.

Between the mind's initial confrontation of the varying and changing events and phenomena, and its magnificent productions through an Einstein's brain is an intricate and enticing web of complicated processes and data. In the web, men come to regard themselves and their fellows in pieces and to accept this self-view and social outlook as the normal state of being men. The nature of the web itself encourages this view. It is not the web, but the sticky strand to which one's mind is stuck at the moment that counts. The mere multiplication of mankind also encourages this outlook. Three billion humans rapidly becoming four and, within this century six, have made society impossible without the massive bureaucratization of intellectual, cultural, political, and economic life. This fact has psychological consequences.

In Orson Welles' film of Kafka's *Trial*, there is a horrifying scene of an office the size of a football field, filled with thousands of workers typing. The sameness of the mechanical act of typing is thunderously amplified by the inhuman cackling of a million metal keys beating against the hard rubber rollers. The metallic roar is something from another planet, and the creatures manipulating the machines are living things we barely recognize. But the important thing is what we do see in them: shadows of recognizable creatures, shadows of civil servants sitting at rows of desks in ugly gray buildings, shadows of the academics sitting in departmental meetings, shadows of clerks behind counters who may be found at night sitting alone in lonely city cells.

The headline reads "254 VIETCONG KILLED IN NEW BATTLE." The announcement on the campus bulletin board says "FACULTY VOTES NEW THREE-HOUR LANGUAGE REQUIREMENT." In the jam-packed subway or in the long cafeteria line, what does it mean?

Meaning begins with observation. Man's sensory apparatus is the beginning of his being. The problems of perception—not so much the mechanics of how the senses observe impulses and convey them to the brain, but what happens to these impulses when they enter the complex of the brain —are among the most intriguing challenges to modern psychology. Perception is a concept which binds together the dynamics of how we think with how we create and act. Experience is the catalyst for intellectual and artistic results. But many of the significant experiences from which people learn do not occur within the confines of the institutions whose declared purpose is formal learning. Teachers, professionally educated and legally certified, often do not direct, influence, or even recognize the most significant learning occasions.

In the organized learning situation, the teacher, the systems designed to support him and what he is supposed to do—the school itself—intervene, and become critical factors in shaping certain kinds of experience. To some extent, a school defines for the people in it what relevant experience is. The institution itself is an experience, controlling learning through the limitations and opportunities it builds into itself and imposes upon the people in it. This is illustrated by the lower schools in the urban ghettos, where the ersatz environment created often collides violently with the environment of family and community life. Often the white and middle-class administrators and teachers who conduct these schools simply do not recognize the relevance of the experience fields through which the children move outside of school. In these schools there is a communications breakdown, not so much through alien languages as through alien experience. And mere good intentions are usually not enough to repair or overcome this breakdown.

Through technology, opportunities for cultural, social, and economic experiences have been tremendously enlarged and enriched. Technology extends almost beyond imagination the human capacity to observe and perceive, opening up whole new worlds of phenomena which provoke aesthetic and intellectual responses. We see things which literally no human before us has ever seen. We build in ways never before thought possible. Proximity to and use of the machines result in mysterious psychological reactions deep within the folds of the mind, and these reactions spill out onto the painter's canvas or the composer's manuscript in strange and unanticipated new forms. The human entity experiences wholly new sensations of speed and motion, of life itself.

But technology sometimes places almost unendurable new burdens upon the rational and emotional mechanisms of the mind. The use of human muscles takes new forms. Old employments disappear and new ones are required. A superstructure of life regulated by the machines increasingly closes nature out of the daily perceptions of men, and for many the sky, the mountains, and even the flight of a bird are remote or unknown perception experiences. Not only the quantity of work but the very meaning of work is changed. Technology enables man to live longer and to multiply in number, so that the mere ages and quantity of his species affect drastically the relationships among his kind and the quality of his perception.

The advancement of technology and the growth of population have forced a new organization of human resources, altering irrevocably the individual's concept of himself and his relations with his fellows.

Almost every aspect of modern life tends toward institutionalization, which in politics, the economy, religion, and even the arts conditions the opportunity for the expression of self and the understanding of events, places, things, and other people. The mere administration of modern life invades the privacy of the individual and delimits severely the opportunities for making total decisions, diffusing the moral responsibility for the decisions, and often shattering the possibility of enjoying the fruits of what one has decided or created. Institutions become awesome, living monsters, consuming human beings in the administrative juices of their day-to-day operations. Administration by its nature is a team effort, and the team rushes down the field of daily life in a terrible phalanx, bowling individuals over like tenpins. Technology is the natural ally of the institution. Systems for organizing and processing data, methods of modern finance, techniques for market research and organizing and influencing mass opinion, and the machinery for the rapid reproduction of standardized items in great quantities strengthen the grasp of the institution on the most intimate activities of the individual.

In the arts, the institutions have come to play a key role. Patronage is democratized through the fund-raising campaigns of the great museums, orchestras, opera and dance companies, and universities. Audiences are mobilized by them. Publishing houses come to mean light or darkness for the struggling writer. The most casual observation of the cultural institution reveals all of the ingredients of the modern industrial corporation. They consist of buildings and grounds, parking lots and managerial staffs, fund-raisers and promoters—complete complicated administrative organizations of the cultural endeavor. Through their power to mobilize audiences and patronage, they are influential in shaping popular tastes and sensitivities. Through this power they affect in new ways the life of the individual creative artist and the scholar.

There is no retreat from the institutional character of modern life. The organizations through which we work are bound to have an impact on what and how we perceive. To survive in them, our energies are focused on the means of living, on solving or just keeping under control the puzzling relationships the institution imposes on its individual members.

In his Commencement Address at Yale University in June of 1962, President Kennedy said:

> What is at stake in our economic decisions today is not the grand warfare of rival ideologies which will sweep the country with passion but the practical management of the modern economy. What we need are not labels and clichés but more basic discussion of the sophisticated and technical questions involved in keeping a great economic machinery moving ahead. . . . I am suggesting that the problems of fiscal and monetary policy in the Sixties as opposed to the

kinds of problems we faced in the Thirties demand subtle
challenges for which technical answers—not political answers—must be provided. . . . You are part of the world, and
you must participate in these days of our years in the solution
of the problems that pour upon us requiring the most
sophisticated and technical judgment.[23]

The President concluded that from our exercise of "sophisticated and technical judgment" will emerge our new
vision and a demonstration to the world of our "superior
vitality and the strength of the free society."

Perhaps it is inescapable that we should come to speak of
our political, religious, artistic, and personal lives in the
vocabulary of the corporation. Perhaps it is inevitable that
the future of our national experiment must be pinned upon
the sophisticated administration of the new technology. Perhaps the successful, efficient, and smooth administration and
management of our institutions does automatically insure
qualitative results.

But serious ideological issues do remain. They are embedded in the processes of management, control, and administration, and in the impact of these upon the product
of the institution and upon the day-to-day lives of those who
are a part of producing it. The lives of the people who work
in the institutions are often more directly touched by the
operation of these processes than by the significance or
meaning of the products or the services to which the institutions are devoted. Moreover, these processes of institutional
management and administration are charged with political
electricity. Conflicting designs for the distribution, use, and
flow of power are central to the administrative and managerial life of the institution.

Currently popular slogans such as "Black Power" and, in
the academic world, "Student Power" and "Faculty Power"
may be sophisticated symptoms of the institutional realities.
But no one can be quite sure just now what the speakers of

these slogans ultimately want, except *operational* power *within* institutional frameworks.

Black Power advocates have produced a new vocabulary, substituting "Black" for "Negro" and "Rebellion" for "Riot," etc. But except for the assertion of the desirability of possessing and using power in behalf of blackness, the advocates of Black Power have yet to issue significant programmatic manifestos. Even if one acknowledges that disorganized street violence is rebellion, a great distance remains between that and revolution. The black militants have yet to produce a coherent critique of American economic or political values or of the premises upon which lower or higher education in this country are based. What has been produced is a critique of current distributions of power within the going systems— political, economic, and educational. The significance of this critique is its emphasis on the processes of power. The connection has been made between the possession of the important decision-making posts in America by whites and the patently unfair distribution of power as between whites and blacks throughout American society. This unacceptable result has raised very serious questions about the principles through which the political, economic, and educational institutions are organized and operated. The unacceptable *result* has suggested that perhaps the *means* are unacceptable. This critique necessarily puts the words "black" and "power" together. Given the problems besetting both blacks and whites in America, the Black Power concept contains a large measure of realism.

The advocates of Student Power and of Faculty Power seem clear enough about initial objectives. The power they want *is* within the going systems for the management and control of the institutions of higher education. Beyond that, what?

The modern city is a unique focus of the technological and organizational implications of contemporary human life.

The urban combination of talents is the basis for the technology. In many ways the modern city is the most complicated and complete organization yet invented by man. It is far more complicated than the systems developed to invent and produce the bomb or to deliver men to the moon. The modern city presents challenges both to the means and the ends of American life. It compels people to relate to each other differently, both within and beyond the institutions through which they conduct their urban political, economic, and cultural life.

Viewed as a work of art, the city is a kind of physical projection of the possibilities and pitfalls of human thought. From the variety and range of talents a mature city contains, emerges a virile and aggressive environment which redirects the human effort and reshapes the human response. The city evokes over a period of time the evolution of new and startlingly different capacities of perception in its people.

The old academic prejudices collide violently with the new knowledge within the framework of the organizations for education. The old prejudices say that action in the arenas beyond the institutional places reserved for thinking subverts thought and that, even within these places, those who think should be insulated from the exigencies of acting. The old prejudices aim to absolve the teacher-scholar from the responsibilities of the practical consequences of his thought; to relieve his institutions—his school systems, colleges and universities—from some of the most difficult and important responsibilities of *being* in the city.

The old prejudices are sustained by a breed of man to whom the idea of power is repulsive and the idea of academic power, repugnant. He does not want to get involved in the necessity for power to sustain the conditions for thought. Nor does he want to contemplate the powerful consequences of thinking. In the terms of political philosophy, he is neither a conservative nor a liberal. He is apolitical. He wants influence and prestige, but without responsibility. He wants to affect institutional and community decisions, but without getting his hands dirty making them. He wants to be paid well, but without undergoing the embarrassment of exposing his profit motive, his self-interest.

The new knowledge suggests an irrevocable linkage between the organization of the process of thought and the application of thought through action. In discipline after discipline, effective teaching requires an action laboratory. In medical education, the clinical and internship years are critical. The relationship between the medical schools and the functioning hospital is imperative, and more and more nonacademic hospital centers are finding the maintenance of a research complex essential to their day-to-day functions. The practice-teaching components of the college of education programs are proving to be too circumscribed, too little exposure too late.

Starting at the other end of the thought-action line, solutions to the pressing problems arising out of the new technological urban environment increasingly depend upon a close connection between the centers for thought and the arenas for action. Public health and the conquest of disease necessarily must turn to the academic centers for much of the weaponry they require. The battles in the slums must in part be fought on the academic fields of economics, sociology, political science, and psychology.

In many ways, educational goals inspired directly by acute political situations expose most embarrassingly the barren desert between quite proper political aspirations and quite improper educational attitudes and capacities. Ask Peace Corps administrators about the reliability and creativeness of the higher-educational establishment in the design and implementation of this adventuresome program. Read the urgent pleas of the United States Commissioner of Education for the educators to take some modest risks in the suburbs and the slums. Consult the directors of the Job Corps Training Program or the administrators of the various titles of the federal Education Acts in recent years about the educators' response to "crises," invitations to "experiment," or opportunities to act in keeping with the challenging slogans they use to describe their professional commitments.

The organization of our educational systems remains deeply committed to an accommodation of the old prejudices. In the case of our lower schools, this commitment draws the battlelines along which are being fought the key issues of public education. These issues include the idea of Black Power in relation to the idea of Community as a basis for the government of the schools; centralization *versus* decentralization in the organization and administration of the public schools; the validity of the current vogues for measuring academic achievement, especially the importance attached to reading skills and the devices used to measure them; and the unionization of public-school operations at every level—floor sweeping, building, teaching, and administration—as unionization involves the capture and use of power to affect the design and operation of the schools.

The great revolutions of our century do not solely concern the rise and fall of governments. More fundamentally, they concern the fall of man's traditional view of his limitations, and the rise of a renewed elaboration of his possibilities.

The revolutions of our earth satellites illuminate the unfinished revolutions of our minds. Sent into space by a science and technology few of us can explain, the satellite passes equidistant over New York and the remotest village in Vietnam, casting the same shadow over the eyes of professor and peasant. The satellite reduces the most powerful among us to lowly student status. Soaring high above the atmosphere we have polluted together, it reminds its creators that this is a time when we all may be wrong.

The seedbeds of our revolution are new billions living

longer in new cities, possessing mighty new forces which simultaneously arm them for combat in a life-and-death struggle for the spoils, and equip them with a potentially dangerous faith in their own collective meaning and in the inevitability of the eternal survival of the species.

It is sometimes said that man's inventions, his technological capacities, have outstripped his ability to organize, manage, and use them. If this is true, it is a damning indictment of educational systems which have failed to extend themselves to the full measure of their potential.

Our colleges and universities are terribly worried about having overextended themselves. They persist in measuring "extension" by standards at least one century old, and more probably five or six. They are captives of a traditional view of their own limitations.

I do not choose to be a common man. It is my right to be uncommon if I choose. I seek opportunity—not your white paternalistic security. I am not going to be a kept citizen, humbled and dulled by having welfare look after me. I am going to take the calculated risk: to dream, to build and to succeed for myself and my kind.

. . . I prefer the challenge of life to the white, liberal words for it; the thrill of "self-help" for myself and my kind to dependence upon the white man.

I will not trade my freedom to be part of white America, nor my dignity for a white handout. . . .

I could be proud of my country if it gave me reason to be. My first concern is not to be "anti-communist," but how to get myself and my people out of the hell that you call America.

Rioters? Do you mean your panty raiders? If you mean ghetto reprisals then you don't mean riots, but rebellions whose purpose aren't as you say to impress but to show white America that we mean business. . . .

We want what's ours. I am radical enough to care. In fact, I am radical enough to change and to change now.
—Extract from a letter to the editor of a
student newspaper on a community-college
campus in New York City, March 1968

V

Acting in an Academic World

The responsible student knows that a university would suffer irremediable damage if it allowed itself to become embroiled institutionally in a partisan fashion in any subject of current controversy. This is not out of fear that financial or other losses might be sustained because of the stand taken. Such a charge, though frequently made by those who demand institutional alignment, is too ignoble to be considered. The point is that if any university becomes politicalized in this fashion, it will have lost its soul. The essence of a university's being is in its tolerance for all the winds of doctrine, but that tolerance by definition prevents the institution from partisan involvement.

GRAYSON KIRK, PRESIDENT
COLUMBIA UNIVERSITY[24]

Our purpose is to invest in places that are selfishly good for Harvard. We do not use our money for social purposes.

NATHAN M. PUSEY, PRESIDENT
HARVARD UNIVERSITY[25]

THE INTERNAL organization of the contemporary American university, the way it receives and processes the new knowledge and the people who come to it, deepen the schism between thought and action, and encourage the isolation of the academic community from the dynamics of the city.

The superblock campus, the academic "inner city," is organized around the twin principles of *Time Scarcity* and *Knowledge Monopoly*. These principles operate against the mobility of students and teachers in the academic community, against the promotion of a variety of significant alternatives from among which meaningful choices could be made. These principles are hostile to student and faculty participation in the important decision making of the university and to the legitimacy of controversy in the academic community. A campus whose talents and resources are organized on the bases of scarcity and monopoly will not champion those qualities upon which a city mentality depends.

The Time-Scarcity principle maintains that there is simply too little time and too few resources to accommodate the expectations about what the universities are supposed or claim to do. What they actually do, therefore, is wrapped up neatly in tight, temporal packages—two, four, six or seven-plus years big. A union label—the academic degree— is stamped on the packages at the end of the educational assembly line. The value of the degree is measured by the special academic currency system whose basic unit is the "credit hour." Extending the Time-Scarcity concept (and certainly not as an accommodation of the unskilled labor needs during the summer planting and harvesting season), the "academic year" is nine rather than twelve months long. Four of these years are divided into 120 (give or take a few) credit-hour currency units. On a semester scarcity scale, this amounts to 30 units per academic year (nine months), or 15 units per semester. A typical college "course" is three units. This division of time by work units presents a serious problem: how to divide the totality of the subject matter of a formal education into 120 pieces distributed among the various classifications of knowledge within the framework of a political system which is departmental. This is just the kind of problem from which great configurations of political and/or economic power may be developed. The problem concerns the distribution of scarce resources. It is pregnant, therefore, with rich reward-and-punishment possibilities. It invites wheeling and dealing—transactions in power.

Contemporary and often transitory views of what education is and/or what is "important" educationally are decisive in the division of these academic spoils. At the outset, the 120 credit-hour units must be apportioned among the major subject-matter wards and precincts. In the undergraduate realm, these always include the physical sciences (and mathematics), the social sciences, and the humanities (including foreign languages). To these, depending upon the boundaries of the particular realm, undergraduate professional educational components may be added. Each of these asserts credit-hour claims of its own, notwithstanding the reliance by each upon elements of the universal three.

Although all enter the fray armed with arguments about tradition, liberality, integrity, universality, durability, and primacy, external current events are influential in the results at any particular point in time. A national shortage of engineers, nurses, or computer technicians will have an impact. Over recent years the physical sciences generally have enlarged their share of the whole. But as the size of the whole is more or less fixed, the growth of one sector heralds a necessary contraction of others. In general, the humanities and selected social-science precincts have receded.

Assume that the social sciences emerge from this stage of the process with an allocation of 40 of the 120 possible credit-hour units. Each precinct within the social sciences—history, political science, economics, sociology, etc.—must now struggle for its fair share of the 40.

Assume that the historians obtain 15 of the units assigned to the social sciences. Then, at their own departmental table, they must carve appropriate pieces of the 15 for distribution among the specialties in that family. So many units are handed to European History, so many to American, to Ancient, to Modern, to Far Eastern, to Western Civilization. Finally, among each of these categories, still another apportionment must be achieved. In the American History serving, how many study hours are to be given to the Colonial Period, to the Federal, to the Jacksonian, to the Civil War, to Modern, to U.S. Domestic, to U.S. Foreign?

At the end of the road of these negotiations some eager Ph.D., fresh out of graduate school with a doctoral thesis based on some hitherto unpublished letters written by General Pershing, and with a passionate intellectual interest in American diplomatic history covering the period of April 18 through November 7, 1918, discovers—if he is lucky—that every third semester two credit-hour units have been set aside into which he may pour out his scholarship and intellectual passion for the benefit of any students who may show up. Between these periods, he will probably be assigned to teach the introductory freshman three-credit-unit course—a lecture survey of American events from 1609 through the Civil War; second semester: Reconstruction through the Atom Bomb.

Internal academic power politics is intimately related to this process. Success in the competition for the credit-hour units leads to prestige and affluence at the departmental (precinct) level. The larger the allocation to a given department, the larger the teaching staff required to service the units obtained. The larger the staff, the larger the departmental budget. The larger the budget, the greater the prestige of the precinct captain, the chairman—and the more his voice may count at the college (ward) level where the policies for the whole realm are shaped. Ward leaders (deans) cannot proceed far down any policy line without the support of the major precinct captains—although many

ward leaders achieve their own ends by pitting the precinct
bosses against each other and by hedging in large and powerful sectors, such as the physical sciences, with coalitions of
precincts drawn from, say, the humanities and the social
sciences.

Thus the harvest of centuries of learning is fragmented
into bits and pieces in order to fit the demands of the academic packaging system. Knowledge is stuffed into the neat
degree containers. The academic calendar relentlessly establishes the boundaries of the courses, which are the little
partitions inside the packages designed to hold each piece
of civilization in its proper place during shipment. The
credit-hour system arbitrarily evaluates the past, assigning to
it contemporary relevance. Soon the manufacturers are more
intrigued by the process of packaging than by the product
itself. In their zeal to get everything represented inside the
package in time, they succeed in imprinting upon the minds
of the student consumers that the ultimate consumption reward is not necessarily understanding or learning, but conformity to the system at the center of academic political life.

Paradoxically, the principle of academic Time Scarcity is
a direct function of a tremendous knowledge surplus. A curricular system based upon this principle does not provide
enough receptacles to accommodate the productivity of the
human enterprise. The tension between the plethora of
things to know and the enforced shortage of time in which
to study them irrevocably establishes the conclusion that no
man can know very much. A small liberal-arts college, designed to serve between 500 and 1,000 students, will offer
anywhere from 300 to 500 course alternatives over a typical
four-year cycle. The bulletin of a large university with a
student body of 20,000 or more may list more than 2,000
courses. In the typical four-year undergraduate cycle, the
student has the opportunity to enroll in from 36 to 44 courses.
Obviously, his exposure is limited.

The drawback of a limited exposure is translated by the system into a virtue. An "educated man" is defined not by the universality and breadth of his knowledge exposure, but by the limitation and specialization of it. Winding one's way through the labyrinth of all the courses temptingly offered by an institution to the discovery of the 36 to 44 which fit the individual student is simplified by the basic choice of an area of knowledge specialization. The student is usually encouraged to move toward this one fundamental choice as early as possible in his academic career. Having made the choice, he is then urged to move as aggressively as he can to develop a monopoly claim to the body of knowledge defined by his choice. Both the students and the teachers are encouraged to establish Knowledge Monopolies. The most respected teachers are those whose monopolies are strongest. The best students are those who show promise of mastering the faculty's game of monopoly.

Historians may join each other at the luncheon table in the faculty club. If a European historian sits next to an American specialist, a tacit understanding immediately comes into operation that each is the expert in his field and may speak authoritatively about it without challenge from his colleague. Relatively few serious conversational bridges can be thrown across the gap that separates them. The expertise of each is the basis of his professionalism, and the self-respect of each depends in part upon the careful cultivation of the reality (or illusion?) of subject-matter monopoly. These conversational encounters are sometimes relieved by resort to neutral topics such as baseball, where the acknowledged amateurism of each establishes an intellectual parity; or the maladroitness of the university's administration—a subject about which every faculty member is a presumed expert.

The spirit of monopoly based upon the fragmentation of the whole reduces academic conversation to the most common denominators. On some campuses, an entire faculty may add up to One Whole Educated Man. Each member individually is consumed by the inexorable demands of the tenure and promotion system and by the never-ending defense of his monopolistic position. Perched in an uneasy balance between the research and the teaching pursuits, the faculty member's progress depends upon how high he can build the wall around his speciality, publish within it, and confound his colleagues by demonstrating their ignorance of it. Armed with his fellowship, research grant or contract, he may occasionally venture from behind his wall for a year abroad, a brief sojourn in the nation's capital, or for a consulting sortie on the industrial front. But behind the wall or in front of it, he has discovered that it pays to be a splinter of a man—a sharp, deeply penetrating splinter.

The most fashionable function of the academic splinter is to lodge itself strategically in the most vulnerable part of the academic administration. In most meetings of the faculties, most of the discussion is aimed at this target. Faculty group discussion of the content of the curriculum—the implications of the subject matter of what is taught—is extremely dangerous, and is avoided whenever possible. Such discussion threatens monopoly power, disturbs treaties laboriously negotiated to accommodate the credit-hour currency system. Any proposal for a new academic program quickly upsets the faculty forum. A rearrangement of the subject matter over a sequence of courses challenges existing monopolies and immediately raises questions about credit distributions. A proposal to terminate a course is doomed to failure unless the department offering the course proposes the adjustment—something that almost never happens unless that department believes it has something to gain on another credit-hour front.

Consequently, most faculty meetings are devoted to complaints about low salaries, inadequate office and parking facilities, and various aspects of the university's poor relations with the rest of the world. Allegations of the obdurate stupidity, inefficiency, malpractice, and simple inadequacy of the university's administrators are the cement which hold most faculties together. In fact, the faculties and their leaders both understand that much of the charm of academic politics depends upon sustaining the ongoing contention between administration and faculty. Both sides seem to believe in the old academic saw that it is the university president's privilege to talk, the faculty's function to think, and that the faculty ought to do all in its power to keep the president from thinking, just as he would hope to keep the faculty from talking too much. The unfortunate outcome, however, is that all too often there is a torrent of talk and a drought of collaborative, constructive thought.

Our universities, organized around the principles of Time Scarcity and Knowledge Monopoly, produce courses which have become crowded tenements, curricula which are confused and noisy slums. A premium is placed upon knowing a lot about a little, and the successful scholar becomes in effect a monopolistic slumlord—keeper, inviolate, of a vertical knowledge walkup, uninterested in and ill-informed about the other tenements on the curricular block. Faculty meetings are like street-corner protest demonstrations, with the demonstrators often speaking the inept language and adopting the misguided policies of those against whom they protest. The community of scholars takes on the appearance of an intellectually segregated ghetto. And the students— like the children of all ghettos—end up being miseducated or dropping out.

The faculty in the university, threatened by the various parts of its collective self, resentful of any outside tampering with the conditions it has established for monopoly, precludes for itself an overall view of what it is doing or where it is going. Through the self-imposed isolation of its members, its internal disunity, and its superior attitude toward what it imagines the academic administrators do for a living, the faculty has successfully retreated from the fields of power which are often the decisive staging grounds in the life of the university.

The academic administrators, led by their chief of staff, have occupied these fields. They possess the power to rule, but under conditions which discourage among them any incentive to reform. If they preside skillfully over the status quo and regard the education of the young lightheartedly; if they resist the temptations to contest the main thrust of American life, and embrace and dignify the conduct of the others who possess power in our society, they themselves may enjoy a unique prestige and status.

There are varying views of what an American university president is or should be. Clark Kerr has described multiversity's president as a "leader, educator, creator, initiator, wielder of power, pump; he is also officeholder, caretaker, inheritor, consensus-seeker, persuader, bottleneck. But he is mostly a mediator."[26] Before he rose to the presidency of the University of California, Dr. Kerr had a distinguished career as a mediator of labor disputes.

Before he became president of Cornell, James Perkins was a foundation executive. According to him the university president is

> concerned with the institution as a whole, the activities it supports, the public face it presents, and the private concerns with which it is occupied. This job cannot be divided among the disparate elements of the university. It is the president and others with managerial responsibility, cooperating with faculty and student leaders . . . who must be concerned with the apparatus of the university and with the idea it represents. . . . Few large faculties have been able to provide this leadership for themselves.[27]

One may ask how many university presidents would agree with the regent at the University of Minnesota, who, during that institution's search for a new president last year, commented that the university leader must be religious "but not domineering about it." And he certainly "can't be political."[28]

The American university president performs a very special brokerage function for the academic club. He mobilizes money in the public and private marketplaces. To raise the money, he must converse with the publics who possess and control it. To be understood, he must converse in the language they understand. To do this, he often assumes popular poses and personifies values somewhat different from those his faculty intends or pretends to respect.

Presidential survival frequently depends exclusively upon raising money and, once it is raised, upon the skillful management of its expenditure. The president is supposed to direct the building program, collect tuition, raise salaries, allow for retirements, deduct withholding and health-insurance assessments, operate hotels, restaurants, and hospitals, pay the electric and phone bills, and account accurately for everything. He must originate a magnificent ten-year plan and package it in an inspiring and visionary ten-minute speech. And his blueprint for the future must marshall the belief and confidence of the laymen to whom he presents it, while making it clear to his faculty that he's only kidding, i.e., "raising money." He must be seen breaking ground and cutting ribbons with mayors and governors, sipping tea with society matrons, and hobnobbing with the boys at the right clubs—Rotary and Athletic.

Observing presidential conduct, most faculty members profess horror or disgust, though many are undoubtedly secretly envious. The world at large, with horror or envy, awe or contempt, regards the university president as his faculty's intellectual leader—an embodiment of academic wisdom and virtue, the spokesman for the whole institutional enterprise.

The American university presidency has produced some extraordinary promoters and fund raisers, some able builders and businessmen, and, if one counts General Eisenhower at Columbia, one chief executive of the United States since Woodrow Wilson. It has also produced an office in which actual leadership power seldom extends to the main business of a university. Consequently, it has become an office through which few educational statesmen have emerged.

The pressures of its operational responsibilities discourage the administrative leadership of a university from thinking about the content of higher education. Nothing is more dangerous or politically perilous than an administrative venture into the labyrinth of faculty ward-and-precinct politics. Consequently, most academic administrations either reluctantly tolerate or actively support the Time-Scarcity and Knowledge-Monopoly principles.

Moreover, social criticism is an academic course fraught with political peril. It simultaneously arouses the academic prejudice about the disconnection of the university from the controversial tumult of the world surrounding it and plows the soil for the alienation of public bodies and private philanthropists. Most university presidents have discovered that it is far better to be religious without being fanatical, political without being partisan.

Such a position has much to commend it. It is not unlike that of the wife in the popular anecdote who leaves all the important things in life to the management of her husband— things such as atom bombs, space flights, and China policy— reserving to herself the unimportant things such as the monthly paycheck, the rearing of the children, and the management of food and shelter.

The academic managers congregate their substantial powers around the formalities of the system. Tremendous energy is poured into the design of the master campus plan. Faculties are artfully led into a quagmire of complicated schemes for the revision of the academic calendar into trimesters or octomesters; or for launching oceanographic centers or paramedical institutes or other ventures which hold promise of strengthening and extending the existing monopolies while also adding to the sum total of what must be "administered." Each proposed innovation implies an extension of the managerial bureaucracy. And, because academic life is so complicated and the institution is growing so large, the direction of the whole naturally requires a more active leadership at the center—a centralization of managerial power.

The formula is simple: On the inside, encourage the faculty to play the game they seem determined to play. The conclusion of that game is confusion, powerlessness, and frustration. On the outside, threaten no one. Go down the middle of the road, avoid notoriety, and tell the board of trustees what they want to hear.

University trustees like to hear what they want to hear. An invitation to serve on the board of trustees of a university is an invitation to exchange goods. Through the invitation, the institution seeks the prestige of association with a "leader" and, hopefully, the exercise of his leadership power —usually economic or political—in its behalf. The captains of industry and political magnates are much in demand for the jobs. The candidate, on the other hand, will find the invitation flattering if colleagues on the board are, in his estimate, as distinguished or more so than he, and if the institution to be governed is itself distinguished, or potentially may be. Most trustees accept the position under the illusion that universities are relatively calm places and reasonably simple to govern, especially when compared with the government of a large industrial corporation. The heat of the profit motive is not supposed to be present. There are no distressing stockholder meetings in the offing. And Education, like Motherhood, is one of the few areas left in American life that one can support whether he is a Democrat or a Republican, a banker or a labor-union potentate.

A good trustee is supposed to use his political drag or connections in behalf of the institution he agrees to serve. He is supposed to give money from his personal fortune and persuade others with dollars to contribute them. He is supposed to tell the academic management whatever stock or real-estate market secrets he knows which may strengthen the holdings or aspirations of the university. And, when asked, he is supposed to reveal managerial knowledge which may be useful to the administration of the educational institution.

He expects the institution, on the other hand, to be the best of its kind and to operate efficiently. He expects the board position to provide him with some interesting and perhaps fruitful associations, and some interesting, noncontroversial subjects to think about.

Some governing boards meet once a month during the academic year. Others meet three or four times a year and some only once or twice. Many convene off the premises of the institution. Few encourage intimacy or even acquaintanceship with the faculty or students in the enterprise to be governed. Consequently, an understanding of what being the "best of its kind" or "efficient" means is usually the result of what the academic administrative leader—the president —tells the board is "best" and "efficient."

Board meetings are usually staged around eating occasions. They are times for conviviality and the exchange of gossip. In most institutions, the typical board meeting is three to five hours in length. Sometimes, in institutions where they are held more infrequently, they last for a full day and include visitations to the sites of new or proposed buildings, and carefully directed "seminars" or committee sessions which expose board groups to selected members of the faculty and the student body. Through these role-playing sessions, board members are "kept in touch."

Agendas for board meetings are always long. Because

of the corporate nature of the university, agendas invariably include items pertaining to large sums of money, major construction undertakings, and involved personnel matters. The dockets are supported by thick volumes of detailed materials, explanatory information seldom read by busy board members before the meetings. Agenda items containing the slightest potential for conflict are usually resolved informally among an influential few before the formal meeting convenes. Meetings of boards—even of the public institutions where the membership is elected by popular vote—are seldom marked by open disagreements or honest debates, and almost never by the exposure of disagreements between the board and the academic administrators who, in theory, are responsible to it. Among the private universities, most boards meet in closed session. The students and the faculties are seldom aware of the fact of the meeting or its location.

Public and private academic institutions in this country are chartered by the states in which they are located. Boards of trustees are creatures of the legal fact that universities are corporations. By the laws of most jurisdictions, there are virtually no limits upon the powers of a university board. It is sovereign with regard to property, money, and personnel. It is responsible finally for the activities and programs of its institution. The administration and managerial officers of the university are employees of the board. The faculties are not self-governing. They, too, are employees of the board of the corporation. To the extent that they enjoy any autonomy, it derives from privileges granted, not from powers vested. In some universities, schemes have evolved through which "many broad and crucial powers of educational decision—including the choice of teaching staff and the control of the curriculum—have been . . . delegated to or left in the hands of the working faculty."[29] In the normal course of a university's affairs, boards have neither the time nor the inclination to intrude into the intricacies of faculty politics.

But in the tough cases—which are almost always controversial and precedent setting—where normal faculty and
administrative processes fail, boards do not hesitate to
plunge in with firm answers to complicated curricular and
academic personnel problems.

Among the public institutions, boards are either elected
by the people or appointed by a public executive for set
terms. In the private sector, with very few exceptions, the
boards are self-perpetuating.

Every trust has a beneficiary—every trustee, a fiduciary
obligation. The terms of a trust must state its purposes. The
operation of fiduciary principles in the academic corporation
is unique.

The purpose of an academic trust is the management of
corporate assets in behalf of "education"—about the meaning of which the academics themselves often disagree. To
whom are the trustees of a university responsible? For whose
benefit do they hold properties, direct the expenditures of
large sums of money, and make decisions about what education is or should be?

In the industrial corporation, managerial *consensus* harnessed to the purpose of profit making links the responsibilities of a board of directors to the stockholders. But in
the academic corporation, the presence of *controversy* is a
prime indication of institutional health, and the enterprise,
by definition, is not for profit. Universities, public and private, it can be argued, are infused with public purposes, and
the governing board, brought into being by the state, is
responsible to "the public" for its conduct. But what public,
and held responsible how?

Board government in our colleges and universities has extensively deteriorated into despotism in a few extreme cases.
Far more common, however, are boards that are ineffective
and largely irrelevant to what goes on in the university. Even
if these boards had the desire to govern their institutions

effectively—and many do not—they have congealed into a homogeneity of interest and power unresponsive to the tasks of academic government.

The academic institutions have grown into large and complex corporate enterprises. In New York City alone, for example, there are at least three universities each of whose annual operating budgets exceeds $125 million, each with more than 1,000 employees on its payroll. Few boards under present conditions are equipped or prepared to handle with intelligence the implications of these magnitudes. Just as the faculties have abdicated large and significant powers to the academic managers, so have the boards of trustees. A somewhat skillful university president can usually lead his board to any conclusion he wishes. He has privileged access to them and to the relevant information which should concern them. He is a board's main boulevard to the "truth."

A balance of power between the administrator and the trustees is further subverted by the changed character of philanthropy. Trustee influence based on the large private gift has declined simply because there are few Rockefellers, Fords, or Carnegies left in America to make the large bequests to the universities. Private philanthropy has been decentralized and, proportionately, it has become a smaller part of the whole. Public "philanthropy" has moved front and center stage. The federal, state, and municipal governments are the largest patrons of higher education in the United States, and as a rule the influence of board members is not crucial in tapping these sources of money.

In advertising themselves, our universities do not stress the commercial-industrial, property-owning, corporate aspects of their personalities. Indeed, quite the opposite: they go out of their way to avoid the nuts-and-bolts, dollars-and-cents, landlord-and-tenant images. For quite obvious reasons they deemphasize the basically autocratic nature of their self-government and play down the relationship between the administration of money, property, and law, and the atmosphere of freedom so imperative to any educational effort.

But our universities do claim to be *centers* for learning, for education for freedom. They stress their existence as *communities*—campus and geographic, professional and scholarly, free, and thus *politically committed* to a particular version of community organization.

Much of the scholarly work and community life of a university goes on outside the classroom—important and central as what goes on there is or should be. For better or for worse, our universities *are* communities, communities in which freedom, or its impairment, is the decisive condition affecting all the rest.

The government of a going community consists in the delineation and administration of rights and duties, justice, relationships among individuals and between them and the public authority of the community, and between the community and the rest of the world. These are also the objects of university government.

The ground rules of campus life are elaborate in the regulation of the affairs of students and teachers, curriculum and social life, economic, cultural, and political activities. The statutory law of the university is printed in thick volumes— student manuals and faculty handbooks. These are among the first printed things handed to students and to faculty when they arrive on campus. There is no such thing as an apolitical government. The government of a university, like the government of any community, is political. If it is to be honest government, it must be regarded politically.

The politics of university governing boards—the interplay of power between trustees and administrators and the domination of the decisions of the former by the power of the latter—are autocratic and anachronistic in the American setting. How paradoxical it is to bring the cream of our youth

and the best of our scholars together for the explicit purpose
of Education for Freedom in communities purposely organ-
ized on anti-freedom principles!

The government of our country's colleges and universities
is ripe for reform. The reform must be along cooperative and
democratic lines, recognizing that, in a community devoted
to the discovery of knowledge and the application of reason,
those to be governed should govern themselves. The government should be based upon the representation of the relevant
constituencies, balanced to encourage honest debate and the
full disclosure of the salient facts operative in the community's life. These political responsibilities should be shared
by students, faculty, administrators, and members of the
major communities a particular university purports to serve,
to which it is related.

The alternative to such reform is more intensive regulation
from beyond the academic community—the imposition of a
more aggressive external public authority—or the perpetuation of a management-dominated trustee autocracy.

In the defense of administrative power, the academic managers exploit the atmosphere of autocracy permeating trustee
government and the principle of Knowledge Monopoly so
central to faculty politics. The vital information upon which
intelligent decision making in the university must be based,
flows directly into the offices of the administration. Sensitive
data about the student body and the faculty, most of the
vital knowledge about the economic and material life of the
institution, and the kinds of information essential to judgments about the quality of operations collect and congeal
in the administrator's hands and eventually become the private preserve of the chief executive. In any debate with the
faculty or the students, the administrator begins with the
tremendous advantage of privileged access to this knowledge. In any confrontation with a board of trustees, this is
the administrator's primary weapon. In any relationship

with audiences beyond the campus, the administrator decides what to tell and what to withhold. Much of the campus tension between the administrators and the faculty and students centers on efforts by the latter to find out what the former knows. Much of the serious difficulty which the foundations, the federal government, the state legislatures, and the municipal public authorities confront in their relationships with the academic institutions flows from the unwillingness of the university administrators to disclose the relevant and vital information.

The virtue of full disclosure is, of course, first on the list of virtues a university champions. Scholarship, supposedly, is based on a free trade of ideas, upon sharing knowledge freely. This principle is widely dishonored by the administrators of the scholarly institutions in the defense of the power of their offices.

The spectacular growth of administrative power in the university facilitates the centralization of institutional decision making; and the centralization of decision making accelerates the growth of administrative power. Centralism is defended on the grounds of efficiency and with the argument that those who teach and study are so busy teaching and studying they cannot and should not be bothered by the complicated, overriding problems of the university's life. One is reminded of the arguments in favor of industrial monopoly at the turn of the century; and of the assurances Adolf Hitler once gave to the German people that, if they would but fully relinquish the political and economic affairs of the land to him, they would have the energy and time through his New Order for the release of their greatest scientific and cultural creativity.

The older arguments for centralism in industrial organization extended to the savings and efficiency allegedly to be gained through the centralization of the purchase of the materials for production, of the manufacturing effort itself, and of the distribution of the product. The General Motors model for accommodating very large size—the simulation of competition among semiautonomous units within the corporation—suggests that there may be a point of no return in the theory that relates size, central control, and efficiency. It suggests there may be such a thing as being too big. We really have no way of telling now whether the G.M. formula is "efficient." The disconnections between making profit and being efficient have progressed too far, and, with regard to the automotive industry, the concept of efficiency is now much too qualified by noneconomic factors—by chrome and fashion and monopoly. But as multicampus universities, public and private, have become commonplace and large central campuses with semiautonomous colleges numerous, General Motors is sometimes advanced as an appropriate model for the organization of units in the education industry.

To the extent that many of the functions of educational management and operations have become computerized, centralization for some managerial purposes may be defensible. The statistical work of the admissions office, the registrarial operation, the recording of grades, the scheduling of classes, the utilization of space, the processing of employee records—these may now be programmed by the machines under the direction of a central management. There are certain kinds of materials used in the educational enterprise which may be purchased and distributed more economically through a single center in a large and diverse institution—especially if the institution really relies on competitive bidding, which many don't. Some savings may be possible through the centralization of academic architectural and building operations—at the risk of accepting standardized results. But once one moves beyond these operational processes and the purchase of materials to the key "manufacturing" and "distribution" functions of the educational enterprise, the virtues of centralized organization may be quickly converted into dangerous vices. The standardization of curricula, the packaging of courses, the attempt by remote control to make the social and cultural life of various campuses conform to some abstract, homogenized standard, the effort to govern academic communities from a distance—all of this is subversive of the educational process. Neither efficiency nor the call for institutionalized "unity" justify the common administrative propensity to preclude controversy, reduce competition, and impose some master consensus upon the form and the content of the confrontation between those who teach and those who are taught. The production of educated men and women and the distribution of knowledge are not like the production and distribution of automobiles.

There has been a massive retreat from thought and action about the heartland issues in organized formal higher education in the American university. The nature of faculty politics precludes such thought and action; and they are a real and present danger to those who would defend and extend administrative power. Members of the governing boards of the institutions have neither the time nor the experience nor the knowledge to join the basic issues seriously. The students, most frequently exploited and abused by the excesses of the situation, are generally excluded from meaningful community participation by the powerful faculty and administration Knowledge Monopolies. The majority of the students accept the abuse and exploitation placidly. They sell out young. The activist minority, in the ignorance forced upon it and out of its frustration, often responds to exclusion abusively in the hope of exploiting the system.

The forms and formalities of the educational organization and process dominate university thought and action about itself as an institution. These are detached and isolated from the tough problems of value and content.

There is no dearth of conflict and controversy on our campuses—but most of it is about irrelevancies. In American

university life, as in the life of our urban centers, a mecha-
nistic and organizational approach to the salient problems is
preferred. Behind this approach undoubtedly is the conviction that our superior technology points toward the ultimate
answers and that an elaboration of the bureaucracy is a necessary and desirable accommodation of the technology. Our
universities are now infected and overcome by the conditions they have helped foster in the larger society. Yet, they
deny that they are sick. They confuse the excitement of
growth with a condition of health. Their retreat from the
realities of their own lives is a symptom of their illness.

Ben Shahn, the painter, has written about an interesting
problem in the world of art:

> Form and content have been forcibly divided by a great
> deal of present-day aesthetic opinion, and each, if one is to
> believe what he reads, goes its separate way. Content, in
> this sorry divorce, seems to be looked upon as the culprit.
> It is seldom mentioned in the consideration of a work of
> art; it is not in the well-informed vocabulary. Some critics
> consider any mention of content as a display of bad taste.
> Some, more innocent and more modern, have been taught—
> schooled—to look at paintings in such a way as to make
> them wholly unaware of content. . . .
>
> Content may be and often is trivial. . . . But I think it can
> be said with certainty that the form which does emerge
> cannot be greater than the content which went into it. For
> form is only the manifestation, the shape of content.[30]

Just as it is futile to evaluate the form of a painting apart
from its content, so it is with an evaluation of education.
Among a free and urban people there is an irrevocable bond
between the content of their freedom and the urban form
their life takes. The urban form of American life is the shape
of the content of its freedom. The bureaucratic form of the
American university is the shape of its educational content.

When the institutional forms through which urban life

flows come to dominate the content of that life, the disconnection between value and conduct can be dangerous. In this country the ascendancy of the forms means that the machine and the organization dictate to the man. Not only the machine, but the man becomes automated. Not only the organization, but the man becomes bureaucratized. Those who have the power to decide in the American university have encouraged their own automation. They have not been the innocent victims of bureaucracy; they have been the active architects of it.

The technology and the urban environment place under extraordinary stress the values by which we profess to live. A growing abyss separates the shape of our life from what we say we believe or think we ought to. The content of American life reflects a gnawing doubt about the old meanings and the absence of new ones.

Our universities are organized to resist change. They are fearful of the meaning of it for themselves.

Q. Is this College relevant to the whole upheaval?

A. This College is a glorified high school, in the way that it is concerned almost exclusively with cramming things into students' heads. I see nothing here that concerns itself with the problems of values and the concern of man for his fellowman. . . . I see no relevance at the College. The College has defined its responsibility as preparing students for graduate schools and professional schools and making scores on graduate record exams. It is training students to become competitive in the society that now exists.

Q. What is the first step in remaking this white College in the midst of a black community?

A. One of the first steps is indicated by your question—a white university in the midst of a black community. The fact that we can use words like this in the twentieth century means that we're in deep trouble. . . .

As long as people feel that their particular lives are sheltered and privileged, untouched by the injustices and cruelties of this society, they will hide behind "not knowing." They will accept the symptoms of the diseases of this society—indifference, immorality. They will do something only when the disease really strikes them, when their homes are threatened or when their privilege seems to be toppling. Then they will do something—they'll probably strike back immediately at the people whom they think are the enemy—the vandals, the hooligans, the looters.

This is a sick, sick society in which our educational institutions are chief instruments in the perpetuation of the sickness, in training human beings to rationalize the sickness and to exploit it for themselves.

I think this college is a symbol of a very subtle, and pervasive form of the sickness.

—Excerpts from an interview between the editor
of the student newspaper at City College in
New York and Professor Kenneth B. Clark,
April 1968

VI

Learning and Survival

The unemployment rate among Negroes has been double that among white workers ever since the Korean War, but federal figures . . . show an abrupt widening of the gap. . . . White joblessness has gone from 3.5 percent to 3.8 percent; Negro joblessness has climbed . . . from 6.9 percent to 8.8 percent.

An especially worrisome aspect of this up-surge is that much of it stems from an increase in idleness among Negro teenagers, the group most conspicuous in all the summer explosions. Normally about one-quarter of the Negro youths looking for jobs can't find them; in October [1967] the ratio was just short of one-third. For white teenagers the comparable figure was a trifle over one-eighth.

THE NEW YORK TIMES[31]

Senator Percy (R-Ill.) . . . cited a survey of the Yale class of 1952 which he said showed the typical graduate of Yale 15 years ago is now earning $20,000 a year, with few debts, his own home and two cars.

He quoted the survey as saying the '52 Yale man "is satisfied with the status quo, agrees with the present pace of the civil-rights movement, the present policy in Vietnam and the way the country is going in general."

"I find this totally and completely disturbing," Percy said. "It indicates that the class of '52—and no doubt other classes from the leading colleges—is more concerned with protecting its own affluence and well-being than with improving the condition of the rest of the country and the rest of the world."

THE NEW YORK POST[32]

A RECENT study of the problems of educational systems in the great cities of the world concludes:

> It is useless, and indeed, it can be dangerous to look on education as an entity in itself or as taking into account only the psychological and social needs of the child as an individual person. The phenomena of the educated unemployed are a steadily growing illustration of the danger of such a point of view. To provide "education" without considering at the same time how children endowed with this "education" are to use their knowledge and skills in the community is to plan for tragedy. In recent years events in many United States cities, in Tunisia, in the Philippines, in Ghana, in Egypt, and all over Latin America—the examples could readily be multiplied—are evidence that educational systems not geared to employment can lead to disaster.[33]

Everywhere on this planet higher and higher levels of education are required in order for people to make a living. The technology intricately interweaves social and economic policy making with educational planning and policy making. The resulting tapestry has a political coloration. This is especially true in a country such as the United States, whose technology is most mature and whose political value structure presumes an intimate relationship among economic well-being, social class, and effectiveness of political participation. A university in this country which claims that it is planning for *its* future apart from the explosive economic, social, and political controversies current in American life is deceiving itself, and through such self-deception may mislead the public about its purposes as well as its day-to-day conduct.

If we Americans ask, "What is an Educated Man?," the first chapter of the answer *must unequivocally take account of what a man must know in order to survive in an economy destined to become even more complicated than ours now is.*

Of course, the objectives of higher education transcend the preparation of people for economic survival. But to equip men for such survival is a basic and indispensable element of a completer statement of the purposes of education, higher and lower.

In the United States we would expect hardly anyone to argue with this proposition. The economic purposes of education are deeply embedded in our own tradition, and they, perhaps more than anything else, have produced the unique and innovative American contributions to the process of education. Horace Mann's arguments for universal public education were aimed mainly at practical economic objectives. The landmark Morrill Act of 1862—the basis for the system of great land-grant universities in the U.S.—established colleges and universities "to teach such branches of learning as are related to agriculture and the mechanical arts . . . in order to promote the liberal and practical education of the industrial classes in the several pursuits and professions of life." These institutions were not to exclude other scientific and classical studies, but they were especially meant to feature what Mr. Morrill called "the useful sciences." Americans may very well take pride in their inventiveness, which anticipated by almost a century the central issues in today's debates about the reform of higher education in England, France, the Federal Republic of Germany, and several other European countries.*

---

* In the current debate about the reform of university education in West Germany, that nation's Chamber of Commerce and Industry has argued for limiting the number of students who may enter the universities to ten percent of the qualified population rather than to fifteen percent as is being proposed. In 1966–67 there was a total of 262,000 students in the universities, about eight percent of the eligible-age population in a nation of 60 million. The Chamber is concerned about the creation of an "overeducated society." The Chamber believes that enlarging the university opportunity would have the effect of "devaluing" lower-school education. "If this happens, the economy will be seriously affected in the future because there will

But many academics in this country do argue with these propositions. They argue with them in their professorial roles even though they themselves, through their increasingly organized efforts to improve *their own* income and working conditions within the academic corporations, illustrate the powerful connection between economic goals and educational qualification. They expect their own educational achievement to increase their own earning power, even while they proclaim that this is not properly among the primary purposes of the higher education for their students.

The deep and intense feeling about this matter takes the form of several operational prejudices which get built into the way curricula are designed, academic prestige and status are defined, and the conduct of teachers and students are regulated. To mention a few:

—"Pure" research carries more prestige than applied research, and research generally, more than teaching.
—Subjects which have vague or ill-defined job connections generally carry more prestige than those with well-defined job implications.
—Employment by or enrollment in a four-year college featuring the "liberal arts" and preparation for graduate study carries more prestige than employment or enrollment in a two-year community college in which practical themes dominate.
—Lower- and secondary-school teaching in a suburb, where presumably the majority of the youth are college-bound, carries more prestige than teaching in a ghetto,

---

not be enough technicians and workers who are primarily turned out by the lower schools" at the ages of fourteen and fifteen.

It may be assumed that most of the leaders of commerce and industry in the Federal Republic are products of the old German university tradition—a tradition which continues to have great influence among many American academics.[34]

where the majority of the youth have less well-defined futures.

—Highly specialized subjects which, by the nature of our educational system, are not taught in depth to the majority (physics, mathematics, and, sadly now, philosophy) carry more prestige than subjects which (though they may be equally specialized and difficult to master) are by content more directly related to conditions in which all men are likely to get involved (political science, sociology, psychology, education).

—Full-time academic status (even when held by the less qualified) carries more prestige than part-time status (even when held by the very qualified).

—Campus-oriented institutions generally enjoy more prestige than noncampus kinds of institutions; and residential students generally have more status than the commuters, whose life habits expose them daily to the "outside" world.

These prejudices undoubtedly reflect the wounds and scars accumulated during the long and difficult struggle to free the university from the domination of the Church and the state while at the same time maintaining its independence from what it has traditionally defined as the transitory, self-serving, and often anti-intellectual demands of secular society. Scholarship, it is argued, must define the terms of its own thrust. To tie the learning enterprise to the exigencies of any dimension of the society in which it exists is to run the risk of undermining the independence and freedom upon which scholarly inquiry depends. The great and enduring ideas, by definition, transcend the needs and crises of any particular time and place. The university runs the risk, it is maintained, of being reduced to a mere training service station, into which any special-interest group may come demanding assistance in the solution of its immediate problems.

The university's active engagement in the knowledge problems of the society in which it exists does carry with it very real risks. But in a country where the manpower needs in industry, the professions, commerce, and government are directly dependent upon how the economic objectives of formal education are regarded, disengagement and nonparticipation are even more risky. In fact, disengagement, detachment, and nonparticipation are practically impossible.

The curricula of our law, medical, business-administration, and teacher-education schools are sensitively responsive to standards and criteria imposed from the outside by the practicing professions. Commercial and industrial firms depend almost exclusively upon the colleges and universities for the provision of key personnel and future leaders, and they are encouraged to recruit aggressively on the campuses. The majority of them arbitrarily require a college degree as a necessary executive qualification, and the successful placement of its graduates is one of the proudest sales boasts of the university. Many of our campuses maintain military-training programs which link directly the performance of the university with the education of future military leadership. Perhaps no group imposes its professional prejudices more arbitrarily upon students than the faculties of the universities in the educational preparation of future academics.

The confrontation between the educational power centers and the other major centers of power in society has become inevitable, making the detachment, isolation, or disengagement of the university no longer possible. The issue now concerns the form and educational significance of participation, and to face this issue honestly the old academic prejudices must be overcome. The issue concerns not only the relationship of the institution to what's going on around it, but also the character of the educational programs into which the institution places its students.

The technology upon which the modern economy is based

is in great motion. Few jobs it now produces are likely to endure over a 15- to 30-year work life. The expanding technology and its often frivolous and erratic job implications magnify the importance of conveying the enduring, the unifying, the underlying principles which hold the various fields of knowledge together. But can this educational mission best be achieved in a vacuum, in the abstract, in isolation from the unique discipline imposed by the responsibility of acting, from the laboratories of direct exposure to the way things are?

In the midst of these educational issues, many of our colleges and universities still substitute contrived experience for the real thing and, in the name of a concentration upon the "fundamental" and the "enduring," address their educational programs to the transitory and the irrelevant. What is inherited from the past is best understood in the context of one's current engagement. These institutions distort that engagement.

The growing body of the "educated unemployed" is a real future threat to social stability in many places. The millions of uneducated unemployed in the U.S. are a present danger. They are a damaging and volatile critique of our economy. Because almost half of them are black, their condition is a deeply serious commentary on the fundamental premises of our society. What are we to make of our uneducated unemployed? Either they can be educated to various levels of effective participation in our economy, or they can't. If we assume that they can, then a white-dominated educational enterprise, in collaboration with other white-dominated power centers, has failed. It has failed in the lower schools. It has failed in the higher institutions. If we assume that the uneducated unemployed in our country are not educable, then all of the power centers in America are in even deeper trouble. For then the whole value foundation of American society is rebutted. Then we should stop kidding ourselves and call this phase of the American "experiment" to a close. Then we should strike out in some completely new direction and revise our educational systems accordingly.

Against the backdrop of these alternative lines of thought, the Black Power theme in American life just now may be viewed as a potentially healthy reaffirmation of the American Dream. It is a declaration of the failure of the dominant, nonblack power *systems*, the breakdown of the power distribution *performance* of basic institutions. But it leaves open for future judgment the value structures to which the power systems still claim to adhere. Black Power is a revolt against this society's actions, which are all the more difficult to accept against the background of its rhetoric.

Movements for black-controlled schools or for the radical revision of the going educational systems are based on the assumption that most of the uneducated unemployed can be educated, that once educated they can be employed, that once employed the benefits of the value structure will come to them, and that there is nothing about being black which makes the assumption untenable. If this assumption proved valid through a fair test, the basic values undergirding American society would be confirmed.

The critical reservation is: there may be something about being *white* which makes those who have decision-making influence fearful about testing this assumption. To make the test, the society must allow in advance for major adjustments of operating-institutional systems in order to achieve a dramatic redistribution of power. Will a white-controlled and -directed society do this? Can it organize itself effectively to achieve this quickly? The uncertainties in which the answers to these questions are wrapped make "blackness" a proper, primary political issue in the United States.

The American bias in favor of grass-roots, local control of the educational systems, in favor of the neighborhood school and of universities infused with a public mission and a public responsibility, predates the current demands for ghetto control of ghetto schools. These demands pursue a respectable American tradition. It is not the ghetto's fault that the social and economic direction by the white majority delimits the employment and residential opportunities of the black people.

"Black Power" may be a transitory slogan, a passing tactic shaped to accommodate the shattered hopes of the last decade, and to keep the pressure on. Unorganized and irrational street violence is a function of frustration and powerlessness, and must be understood as such, even as we condemn violence. No alien ideology has yet captured and solidified the action in the streets. No mass black following for the separatists has yet developed. There is plenty of evidence that the overwhelming majority of the country's black people are struggling "to get in"—but "to get in" black, not bleached. The admissions standards of all of the nation's basic institutions are being challenged—not only in education, but also in organized religion, in industry and commerce, and in the professions. The attitude of those who shaped these standards and now administer them—that the standards are "right" and that those who fail to meet them are somehow "deficient"—is being challenged. Finally!

In education—putting aside the effectiveness and validity of the admissions tests, the devices used to measure intelligence and achievement—the deficiencies are in fact deeply embedded in the systems. When one meets the teenage dropouts from the public schools in the ghetto or even the ones who persist, endure, and earn the general high-school diploma, it becomes very clear that the deficiencies are not exclusively in the human, but largely in the systems which produce the human result.

Most of our colleges and universities have moved into this period of national crisis, this time of delicate balance between disorganized rebellion and something worse, with a "business as usual" attitude. By and large they have maintained their old habits, breaching the admissions frontier occasionally with some special recruiting program or enlarged scholarship plan—but beyond this, nothing. Self-righteously they declare that *they* do not discriminate because of race, color, or creed and that *they* cannot be held responsible for the inadequacies of others. And for the blacks who do get in, the reception planned is also "business as usual." In the classrooms, in athletics, in the residence halls, and in the overall campus society, the assumption is generally made that there are no problems.

But, of course, there are problems—not so much with being a minority, but with being a curiosity, that is—a *black* minority; not so much in the formal principles around which campus life is built, but in the disconnection between those principles and life in the larger world to which the campus does or does not relate effectively. To the extent that the American campus *is* a model—and in the name of academic objectivity is an impartial, neutral, and nonparticipating model—the problems of the black collegian are magnified. Then, what can he do? Integrate in a laboratory? Lead two lives—one on the campus and one off? Isolate? Gratefully be an exhibit? Play the game while suppressing his anger? No wonder that an increasing number of highly intelligent black collegians, young men and women who easily meet the academic system's various criteria, are disaffected by the success, restive in the midst of the contradictions between "going to school" and going home, unsatisfied by white-defined "achievement" in classrooms whose doors are tightly closed. The closed doors—black success contained *within* and limited to model white campuses—threaten to separate the young black intellectual from the majority of his people in the ghetto. With all the temptation of academic success in the presence of this threat, the black collegian is forced to face his alternatives. For him, the context of American civilization is not simply the conditions the university serves up under glass *on* the campus. It is in the relationships of the institution through all of its parts, through the exercise of all its powers, to the universe beyond the campus in which black people must live.

To tell the young black who has penetrated the American academic line, "You can't go home again," is to confirm for him that there is something terribly wrong with the terms of the higher education he now obtains. However much he may want to join the middle class, however much he may master the niceties and rituals of its ways, at the end of four years, armed with his diploma and his marketable knowledge, he remains black. Then, at the end of the model campus road—job offers notwithstanding—he still has no place to go except "home"—segregated housing and/or a prejudiced society.

The educated unemployed may constitute a future threat. The uneducated unemployed are an explosive present danger. But the *miseducated employed* wield by far the greatest influence in the conduct of the day-to-day life of this nation.

Millions of Americans have moved through the highest levels of the formal educational systems into the country's strategic command positions. In these positions, they possess and exercise great powers. Through these powers, they reap whatever rewards American life has to offer. The quality of their formal education is rigorously tested by the way the command power is exercised. What are the connections between their formal education and their capacities to command, to realize, and to enjoy the Good American Life?

As American cities have grown larger and life in them more complicated, there are fewer and fewer places to which the citydwellers go for help at the critical moments in their daily lives—at those times when the issues are life and death, pain and illness, or the vital defense of property and treasure.

Being born or dying, keeping healthy or being cured, keeping solvent or planning for future security—all have come to require expert guidance and the performance of highly specialized services by others. The more specialized the services required, the greater is the concentration of the city places where they may be obtained. These places are occupied by professional experts, usually university-educated counselors and advice givers who, at the moment of client confrontation, commit the really important acts of persuasion in the city.

These advice givers are almost always approached by people under pressure. The client goes to them with important and urgent problems in the expectation that specialized knowledge will point to a way out. But while the persuasion posts are occupied by the possessers of special knowledge, invariably the problems presented to them evoke not only the specialized responses for which the expert was formally prepared, but also advice and counsel based on knowledge and wisdom beyond the persuader's proclaimed expertise.

A lawyer asked to draw a will or confronted by a client seeking to initiate a divorce action or to adopt a child is immediately plunged into giving advice and counsel which goes far beyond the intricacies of probate or family law.

While the visitor to the doctor's office is motivated by the desire to get the illness or malfunction cured as quickly and painlessly as possible, the "treatment" usually involves more than a simple exchange of expert information and services for dollars.

Each of the persuasion professions is subject to two rigorous disciplines. One pertains to the subject matter or the content of the profession—the body of *knowledge and concepts* which is the law or medicine. The other relates to the *practice* of the profession.

Practice is an art—always in two parts. One part involves the application of knowledge to a particular situation—the selection of that information which is most relevant to the individual case at hand. The other is the process of defining the case at hand—a process based mainly upon an interchange between the advice giver and his client. This interchange vitally affects the process of knowledge selection. Through it, the "problem" is defined. The problem may or may not be defined accurately. An inaccurate problem definition will lead to the erroneous knowledge selection. How a problem is defined may depend partly on extraneous factors, such as what a lawyer's wife says to him at the breakfast table or how a patient reacts to the receptionist in the doctor's office. But the definition of the problem—the diagnosis—*links* knowledge to practice, *binds* thought to action in the immediate case. The outcome of the expert-client relationship turns in large part upon the process of problem definition.

The persuasion posts represent a concentration of critical advice-giving power in American life and expose the gaps between the functions performed by the key counselors in the city and their preparation for these jobs through formal undergraduate, graduate, and professional education in the university.

The academics who teach and prepare the key counselors and professional persuaders in our society—and who themselves are key persuaders—are uncomfortable and threatened by the linking of knowledge and practice, the bond between thought and action. As professional people, their own conduct is subject to the two disciplines. But they have created elaborate devices to resist and ward off this reality. The result is often a distortion of their professional product, and the creation of a make-believe world to which they go to work every morning.

Central to the performance of any professional service is the simple recognition of and respect for the idea of the client. The existence of the client is the catalyst releasing the flow of knowledge. The mere presence of the client bespeaks the necessity for a relationship, and the relationship points toward a transaction—an exchange. Doctors and lawyers put an exact value upon their knowledge services, client by client. Politicians are always making power exchanges, and they are reasonably frank about it.

The idea of professional conduct aimed at the service of clients is an awkward complication for the academic administrator and the professor. They reject the idea of having clients. Who could their clients possibly be? If they consult on the outside, governments and industries may be their clients. But such consulting is not supposed to be their preoccupation. Publication and the conduct of researches may add to the total sum of human knowledge and scholarship (while simultaneously contributing to the promotion of self), but clients are not abstractions or mere shadows of self, and universities claim to do substantially more than promote publication, research, and faculty members. The suggestion that students may be the primary clients is especially distressing.

Client status implies a fair exchange between the professional who gives the service and the client who gets it. The exchange of money for services is a complete discharge of respective obligations, and this exchange enhances rather than detracts from a relationship of equality. A medical doctor may and usually does give advice beyond his field of specialization, but he would never assume, without explicit permission, a superior authority over other aspects of his patient's life.

On the other hand, the relationship of deans, presidents, division directors, and the faculty to students, is based upon a presumption of human inequality in almost every aspect of life. The biology professor does not base his authority just on his superior knowledge about biology. He bases it on his faculty status, and this, he too often assumes, entitles him to a superior judgment of the student's outlook toward Vietnam, civil rights, food, sex, clothes, and almost everything else.

Tuition is not regarded as a "price" charged for services rendered, but instead as a sort of privileged-club-membership fee. Running a university and teaching are not viewed as professional services rendered to student-clients, but instead as enduring, ongoing club activities to which the members, on certain conditions, may have access.

Of course, the academic corporation does more than grant degrees to its students. It carries forward research. It "serves the public." It conserves knowledge. And it is true that, in the galaxy of all the things it does, among some the education of the students is a low-priority matter, a diversionary complication in the pursuit of more important and interesting purposes. But, finally, the universities do grant the degrees. The student-clients are there. They contribute a large part of the income which helps to sustain those who teach in and manage the academic corporation. The mere presence of these student-clients serves as a reminder of what the professors and the academic administrators must do to survive in this economy. And what they do, the things they honor and value in their own day-to-day conduct on the campus and beyond, do not go unnoticed by the students with whom they associate, who observe their behavior, who see through them something of what it takes to survive in this economy.

Among many in the university, higher education for survival purposes is viewed as irretrievably nonacademic. Survival is a practical matter, and according to some of the educators, the more practical an educational course of action, the less appropriate it is to include it in a university's program. They argue that learning is for its own sake and that therefore the university exists for its own sake. Utilitarian purposes contaminate learning just as practical connections to the world beyond the campus threaten to subvert the university itself. Accordingly, the university must be shored up and protected—not only physically and programmatically, but also in terms of how it accommodates time. The academic view of *educational time* is connected to the prejudice against the practical and a factor in the academic definition of *utility*. The traditional outlook toward time and utility tends to ignore the predicament into which the contemporary college student is put by the new knowledge. The educated free man must achieve a delicate balance between what he knows and uses at any given time and the outlook he brings to the continuity of the process of knowing more. There is a world of difference between saying, "I am educated," and saying, "I am learning." Unfortunately, the main educational theme in the majority of our colleges and universities stresses the conclusion rather than the process and the continuity. By emphasizing the conclusion rather than the continuity, the institutions for higher learning encourage despair in the reception of the new knowledge. They take the position that, because there is too much to know, no one can know very much. Then they make a fetish out of not knowing very much. This fetish begins with the academic superstition about time.

Compulsory public education in the United States now extends over 12 years of a human life. But at the lower end, through the Head Start program and other innovations prompted by the unique educational challenge of the central-city ghetto, additional years are being added. A growing body of research underscores the decisive educational importance of the first five years of human life, and in some of our cities infants as young as one year are being brought into organized educational systems. At the other end of the formal-educational spectrum, even now the average possessor of an advanced university degree does not enter the job marketplace until twenty-four, twenty-five or twenty-six years of age, and this figure is higher for the typical Ph.D. or M.D. Within the next decade we may anticipate the addition of four to six required years of formal education to the present 12.

This fact coincides with and in part is a function of technology's influence upon the traditional meanings of "gainful employment," "work," and "utility," upon the totality of human time spent "earning a living." We are a people conditioned to a hard-rock notion of the importance of jobs at the very time that the hard rock is being crushed between the tremendous pressures of population growth and the impact of machines upon production.

These pressures have the effect of reducing the number of jobs available in proportion to the number of people requiring them, and of changing the content and nature of the work to be performed and thus of the educational preparation necessary to obtain and retain work.

At the portals to gainful employment this state of affairs requires the prolongation of the educational preparation of people prior to entry into the job market, plus an effort on other fronts—as suggested recently by the U.S. Secretary of Labor—to keep our youth out of the stream of employment for a longer period of time.

During the middle years—the period of gainful employment—these pressures point toward a continued reduction of the length of the workday and the workweek, the extension of enforced periods of leisure through longer vacations, sabbaticals, greater sick-leave benefits, etc.

Finally, on the other end, the pressures lead irresistibly to an earlier maturation of the life of the employed. We may expect a more rigid enforcement of the sixty, sixty-two, or sixty-five retirement age, and a rapid reduction of the age commonly accepted for retirement, probably into the fifties within the next two decades.

At the same time, thanks to the medical sciences and technology, the longevity statistics become more sanguine. As human life stretches out, the portion of it devoted to what we now call "work" contracts. Taking seventy-five years as a normal life-span, and raising the age at which we permit young people to enter the job market to twenty-five, while enforcing retirement at fifty-five, we leave about 30 years for gainful employment in the format of three- or four-day weeks punctuated by three-, four- or six-week annual holidays. None of these figures is unrealistic as one looks ahead only ten to 15 years.

The political, social, and cultural implications of these changes are staggering and are bound to have a direct and far-reaching effect upon the way our educational systems regard time and utility. While more intensive and prolonged formal education will be required to equip people for participation in the job market, the period for using this education to earn money will be much shorter. As the problems confronting our country are bound to become more complex, the nonusage of these talents beyond the period of gainful employment will represent an unconscionable and impossible waste.

Higher education generally is not tooled up to anticipate this rapidly changing situation, and most of the crash programs aimed at upgrading the education of youth in black urban communities totally ignore these realities. Designed for quick results and obsessed by the importance of job placement and quick income, the majority of these programs are preparing the young people for jobs that do not now exist or for jobs that will never generate future upward mobility, or for jobs that are doomed by the technology during the next decade or less. Even if these programs succeeded in solving the immediate problems ("cooling" the summers, keeping the young off the streets, providing some immediate earned income), they would set the stage for critical new problems in the not too distant future.

In many ways, the crash programs now being provided for the teenage youth in the black urban communities have the effect of ignoring the future of these young people for the immediate goal of maintaining domestic tranquility. These programs will not deactivate the time bomb now ticking in American society; at best, they will merely lengthen the fuse.

What we face in these communities is thousands of young black people of great potential whose education has been seriously impaired by inadequate and unprepared lower-educational systems. It is true that many of these people reach young adulthood unprepared to engage in any productive, income-producing work. But to prepare most of them now to enter the very lowest stratum of the jobs available in a technologically mature economy is simply to perpetuate America's traditional approach to the problems of economic survival facing her black citizens. Our black people, who have occupied the lower rungs in an American agricultural economy and in an expanding American industrial society, are not now going to be enthusiastic about occupying the bottom positions in an American technological economy.

The educational problems of the young black people in our cities represent a very special challenge to our colleges and universities. Large numbers of these young people must now be prepared to leapfrog over the dead-end, lower-level economic openings into the key professional and managerial command posts in the economy. They must be equipped to do this *notwithstanding* the educational damage done to them in the lower schools, *notwithstanding* the distortion of life experience imposed upon them by growing up in the ghettos.

Our colleges and universities cannot even begin to meet this challenge within the traditional terms of higher education. Within these traditional terms time is distorted, fields of experience limited, relevant urban staging grounds and highly qualified urban teaching talents precluded.

Urban teaching talent may be found in a diversity of places. It is located in the offices of government, the research centers of industry, in the control centers of banking and finance, in the museums, and in the institutional places where the sciences are practiced. It must be mobilized in the time terms which make sense to it, and these terms often dictate that teaching and research must necessarily be interwoven with applied activities, with practice. Urban talent must be mobilized in the places where the tools and treasures upon which it depends are located. There is nothing sacred about academic soil. It is not the only ground from which learning can grow. There are a multiplicity of urban institutions, industrial and government centers where talented practitioners and students may appropriately come together. With the demolition of the Time-Scarcity principle, the student-teacher confrontation for educational purposes may be paced more realistically. But this requires a much looser conception of how talent is to be engaged and the places where it may be employed on the urban landscape.

Student restiveness on campuses across the land is partially a reaction against the insular, detached, and rigid attitude toward higher education so many of our universities represent. These young adults come to the colleges prepared to grow, seeking new connections in thought and through experience—between thought and experience—only to find receptions which underestimate or misjudge the range and significance of their past experience and their capacity to grow.

More and more of these young people will grow up in cities. More and more of the cities in which they grow up are being overtaken by rapid change. The quantity and the character of much of the knowledge they will seek are also undergoing rapid change, as are the values which will guide the uses to which they will put that knowledge. No urban college or university can long ignore the meaning of all this for itself. Neither the expectations of the students nor the thrust of urban life, nor the impact of the new knowledge will permit these institutions to remain the way they have been if they are to be *centers of learning* and if they are to be *free*.

My last semester here! My wife and I can't wait to pick up the baby and get out of this place. This campus gives a person an unreal view of things.

Someone is always around to pick up the pieces. If you need money, you can write home or take a no-interest loan. If you're sick, there's the free student health service. If you're going nuts, there's a whole battalion of psychological counselors.

I know when you're no longer a student, your parents are suddenly broke, interest rates go up to six percent, and doctors—M.D. and Ph.D.—start at $25 an hour. You've got to dress commensurate with your station, and you can't sit on that shabby couch covered with the bright bedspread—the inevitable badge of the student apartment.

But I really want to get out and go to work. I'll probably take the bar examination, but I'm not at all sure I want to spend the rest of my life in the legal profession. I'm not sure I want to spend it in any profession. In fact, the big thing is not just to go to work, but to find out what kind of work I want to do.

—Extract from a letter from a student at
Indiana University, February 1968

I think by far the most important bill in our whole code is that for the diffusion of knowledge among the people. No other sure foundation can be devised for the preservation of freedom and happiness. . . . Preach . . . a crusade against ignorance; establish and improve the law for educating the common people. Let our countrymen know that the people alone can protect us against these evils (monarchical and class rule), and that the tax which will be paid for this purpose is not more than the thousandth part of what will be paid to kings, priests, and nobles who will rise up among us if we leave the people in ignorance.

THOMAS JEFFERSON[35]

As friends used to say of Einstein, he was a genius in mathematical physics, an amateur in music and a baby in politics. . . . The fact that a man knows everything there is to know about enzymes doesn't mean that he knows very much about Vietnam, or how to organize a peace, or the life and death of nations.

DEAN RUSK[36]

SEVERAL practical principles have guided the American university to its present pinnacles of power:

1. *Action contaminates and subverts objective thought.* Formal education depends not upon the connection but upon the disconnection between thought and action.

2. As a disconnection between thought and action is an a priori condition for "education," *the academic institution has no direct responsibility for the reform of the society which it serves.* On the contrary, it must zealously guard its neutrality about the future and confine its activities to an impartial emphasis on the past and a "take it or leave it" accommodation of the status quo:

3. It follows that *the educational process must be isolated and introverted, physically through the idea of the "campus," and in time through the principle of scarcity.* A dynamic environment is hostile to the educational process thus conceived. The urbanization of American life, therefore, is an anti-educational phenomenon. To the extent that the idea of the city represents and compels action and attracts and generates talents which resist monopoly, the city is a danger to this theory for organizing learning.

4. *"Getting an education" must be understood as a special event in time.* It has a beginning and an end. "Getting an education" extends in time over the period required to "earn" the degrees. Most of the schools disclaim any serious responsibility for or interest in the education of humans before freshman status or after university graduation. One enters this collegiate time-span more or less "uneducated" and leaves it more or less "educated." During the interval the institution insists upon consumer detachment. It tolerates few outside interferences with its monopolistic jurisdiction. It says to the world at large: "The university is the exclusive educational producer during a given period of time for a defined consumer class. For these consumers, everything else is secondary and should stop during that time interval." It says to the student-consumer: "Being educated here precludes being educated anywhere else. For the present, being here is living."

These principles project the academic virtues of isolation, detachment, and "objectivity" into an institutional political position:

> The higher educational system operates in a special dimension above and beyond the power dimensions through which almost all other social institutions operate. It is neither power-ful nor power-less. It has some magical source of energy which is neutral regarding power. On the inside people "think." From the outside what may be observed is the organization and institutional form of people thinking. As thinking has nothing to do with acting, it has nothing to do with power. Just as an action-commitment contaminates thinking, so does a power-commitment corrupt the organization of thinking. The academic process is mystically pure, or at least 99.9 percent pure.

This position is asserted in behalf of institutional autonomy and freedom.

Preparation for freedom—American style—is a cardinal, essential purpose permeating our formal educational enterprise from top to bottom. Freedom is a politically charged idea. How do the practical principles around which university power has come to be organized accommodate one of its most basic purposes and commitments—the education of American youth for participation in a free society? How do the university's notions about its own freedom equip it to conduct education for freedom?

Among the first things we teach the very young in our public primary schools is a respect for the flag and for principles of community life derived directly from our form of constitutional government. From the very beginning, the formal-educational system in this country emphasizes the cultivation of the unique capacities of the individual and American expectations about the conduct of the individual in the group. The theme of American freedom pervades the most elementary instruction in the basic skills. The examples and situations used to teach our children how to read, write, and manipulate numbers are uniquely descriptive of American situations and embody conclusions about appropriate American conduct. In many ways, our lower schools are now the real frontlines for the confrontation of the significant urban issues in this country. It has been in the public elementary and secondary schools that the problems of racial integration have hit first and hardest. It has been in these schools that there has been an intensive and honest search for new teaching methodologies, new ways for handling subject matter and for using the new technology. Our children are exposed more and more at the very outset of the educational game to the issues about which their parents are fighting.

By the time our students reach the colleges and universities, there are very few among them who would seriously challenge the fundamental American premises. Few would advocate the abolition of our form of constitutional government or seriously argue for a one-party political system in preference to our bipartisan arrangement. Even most of the student activists who burn draft cards and protest the Vietnam war believe that through their conduct they are fulfilling American responsibilities while also being true to themselves.

At the uppermost reaches of our formal-educational system, where the subject matter is primarily related to preparation for specialized careers, the professional ethics our students are taught, the canons of practice they master, and even the pitch of the subject matter in such fields as economics and psychology are oriented to our value structure and the traditions upon which it relies. It is the rare law graduate who has the slightest reservation about taking an oath to uphold the Constitution as a precondition to admission to the bar of the state where he intends to practice. By the time he reaches that point, he has gotten the message.

Men may be born free, but they are not born with an

automatic mastery of the vital political terms of the place where free men live. The mastery of these terms is the subject matter of a refined and specialized education.

Few professors, academic administrators, or university trustees would argue with the high purpose of "education for freedom." But not all can accept the political content and consequences of such education. Few would resist the idea that *an educated man emerging from our colleges and universities should, if nothing else, be comfortable living with the freedom principles*. But not all would accept the political requisites such an education necessarily involves.

Education for freedom must include an intellectually practical preparation for political life. The political life of people who claim or hope to be free is unique. Education among such a people is uniquely complicated by their aspiration to be free. Freedom cannot be taught in a vacuum. The subject matter of freedom involves disciplines. But the education-for-freedom laboratory is action. Education for freedom requires experimentation. There is simply no substitute for experience in such an education. The laboratory for such an education is the relationship between thought and action, and between the classroom and the communities in which the drama of freedom is enacted daily. If education for freedom is to be relevant, the experiments and laboratories upon which it relies must be relevant.

At the core of the American freedom experiment are the ideas that government should be with the *consent* of the governed, that the people should actively *choose* their way through public and private life, and that *intelligence* should guide the choices the people make.

The critical areas of choice in modern society are economic, political, and cultural.

Economic choices are directed toward earning and spending. Earning depends upon the freedom of access to occupational and professional pursuits, and the power to pursue these once access has been gained. Spending involves the power and the right to enjoy the material fruits of labor and accumulated wealth, the freedom of access to the purchase, retention, and use of the goods and services produced in a complex, advanced economy such as ours.

Political choices revolve around the constitution and regulation of government and those who conduct it, and the power to influence the composition, execution, and administration of law. These choices assume that each citizen will be connected to that process through which right and wrong, just and unjust are determined and understood and, once understood, accepted.

Cultural choices concern the citizen's opportunities for movement economically, politically, and socially in relation to his fellows—the fluidity of status. The testing grounds for these opportunities are in private associations, voluntary associations in public life, the informal government of the family, the assertion of religious belief or disbelief, and in the objects of the use of leisure time.

To make a *choice* is to exercise power. If the choice is an effective one, it alters the status quo, it changes the distribution of power. The technology and the bureaucratic systems developed to contain and conduct daily life have changed significantly the context for making effective choices in the United States. Power has congealed into larger and larger units—both private and public. The capacity of the individual to make effective choices is complicated and limited by this fact.

Not only has power congealed into larger units, but the control of the power is increasingly influenced by the sharp separation of the possession and ownership of wealth and property from the managerial direction of it. Responsibility for the consequences of exercising power is diffused and depersonalized. In the admissions office of a university or in the complaint department of a large retail corporation, an individual's passionate, subjective, immediate and vital self-interest (the decision he wants to effect) encounters a dispassionate, "objective," institutional reception. The representative of the great power center may profess sympathy, love and affection for the petitioner and his cause even while reaching a negative conclusion, a result frustrating the choice the individual wants to make. A negative result is never the immediate decision maker's fault. Invariably it is a consequence of "policy" or "regulations," enacted somewhere else by people who are also not at fault, sanctioned finally by some ultimate authority, an inaccessible board or executive group, which in turn is responsible to the true "owners"—150,000 shareholders or some public agency whose administrators, operating under law, are also not at fault.

In a mass society individual citizens may move through their daily lives less on the basis of active choices than on the passive acceptance of choices made in their behalf from remote decision-making centers. In effect, they "consent" to the remote control of significant parts of their lives.

For those commanding the key power centers in such a society, the ever-present political problem consists of creating a broad consensus, a popular atmosphere receptive to their exercise of power. The more abusive and ineffective their exercise of power, the more difficult is their task of maintaining the necessary consensus. The excessive abuse or mismanagement of power in a free society is supposed to be corrected in an orderly way through the replacement of existing decision makers with new ones. The defense of the status quo by those who hold power is supposed to respect the ground rules for orderly change.

In the totalitarian situation a challenge to the status quo is more likely to be met by an exercise of power to suppress the opposition, to impose consensus through fear.

Consensus, the popular, passive acceptance of remote control, is always more difficult to achieve and maintain among a highly educated constituency than among a relatively ignorant one. It is more difficult to develop consensus among a truly citified population than it is among a rural one. The breakdown of law and order on the campus of an urban university in a free society (in New York City or in Paris) is symptomatic of an extremely dangerous and serious defect in that academic community. It reveals either an extraordinary abuse and mismanagement of power by those who govern the university, and/or a failure to appeal to and cultivate the intelligence of the citizens, i.e., a fundamental breakdown of the educational performance of the institution. A resort to severe public or academic sanction in order to restore the status quo on the American urban campus will in the long run only aggravate and perpetuate the basic causes of disorder. Such sanctions can serve only to legitimatize the abusive exercise of power by those in command and to impose consensus where none in fact exists. An *American* peace can no more be imposed by force on our university campuses than it can be imposed on our city streets.

Persuasion is an imperative art in a country with the pretensions ours has. But in the overlive society the art of persuasion encounters two severe, interacting difficulties. First, the communications technology has changed the nature of persuasion. The impact of the persuader has been tremendously enhanced. One speaker may address at once millions of people. On the other hand, the techniques for communication have thrown artificial barriers between the speaker and the listener, precluding an immediate and direct exchange or rejoinder.

In American life, the misuse of the communications technology may subvert the premium placed on active, wise choice and convert consent from an active to a passive process. Whether the sale of toothpaste, the solicitation of votes, or the education of the young is at stake, the situation is a source of danger.

Second, in a country as big as the United States, formed from a large number of different ethnic, cultural, and racial groups, it is frequently a difficult problem to achieve a real consensus on the public issues. The advanced techniques for remote communication are often used to create the illusion of agreement and consensus where none really exists. When this happens, the healthy conflict and controversy so essential to reaching temporary working conclusions in this country may be damaged. Where people are persuaded to agree to things they do not understand, the meaning of choosing is undermined. Where people are coerced into reaching a conclusion in the name of institutional unity or national harmony, they are encouraged to stop thinking and to surrender their decision-making rights to some ulterior authority, to a political party, to a public agency, or to a university president.

Education in a free society (and in a free university) must emphasize the standards and bases for choosing wisely from among the alternatives, and the process through which intelligence is applied in choosing.

Education in an unfree society (and in a university which is not free) is compelled to emphasize the standards and bases on which the alternatives chosen by the ultimate authority rest and the process through which intelligence may be used to justify and project those choices.

Intelligence is not the full-time employee of freedom. History is full of examples of how the power of men's minds may be harnessed to serve totalitarian goals. Fascist and communist states are forceful, recent examples. In both, the sciences flourished with great success. In the academic year 1940–41 almost a third of the élite SS corps serving Adolf Hitler possessed the highest degrees granted by the great universities of Germany.

There is no particular reason to assume that American academics are any more devoted to freedom than American lawyers, doctors, industrial managers, or welfare-payment recipients. There is no special reason to believe that when the chips go down on the big issues, such as war and peace, or social justice and injustice, that American academics—whose profession is specially connected to the cultivation of intelligence—will be among the first to man the barricades.

The cultivation of intelligence, however, serves the free society in a very special way, and those whose profession is responsible for such a cultivation do enjoy a special esteem among the rank and file.

The competitive character of our society presumes that each man knows what is best for himself and that reason guides his determination of self-interest or the exercise of his consent in the granting of power to experts—the people possessing special intelligence bearing upon an elaboration of his best interests in society. We not only make this assumption about the great middle class; we make it about the people in the urban ghetto who are being encouraged to participate in the government and administration of the poverty programs.

The trouble is intelligence, too, takes on the garb of power and often leads to new distributions of it and inequalities which may subvert individual freedom. When this happens, both the cultivation and exercise of intelligence may be resisted. Popular reactions against alleged élites ensue.

American literature concerning higher education is distinctly preoccupied with the relationship of freedom to the cultivation and exercise of intelligence. The history of the development of educational systems in this country—from Thomas Jefferson's proposal for a university in Virginia through the provisions of the most recent federal laws for education—dwells upon this same theme.

Understanding this connection between intelligence and power is the key to an understanding of the form and content of university life. This relationship is central now to the role of our universities in the larger American community.

It is in the terms of this link between intelligence and power that stock must be taken of what is happening to the young people sent to our campuses "to get an education."

The profound life decisions have yet to be made by most young adults at the age when they enter college. Most are not married. Though they are subjected to intense pressures to make up their minds about future careers, many have not yet decided. Most are just breaking out of the protective shells of their local communities and familial settings. In the past, they came to the campuses mainly from small towns. Now most hail from suburbia and the big cities. The most talented and interesting among them are in a frame of mind to question and challenge almost everything that has gone before.

Young Americans at the ages of seventeen or eighteen are not completely babes in the woods. Most of those who go to college have seen the inside of middle-class American homes —their own and their friends'. They know what goes on there and vicariously, if not through direct experience, they've made some pretty extensive observations of life— of marriage and divorce, sex, liquor, money, dope, and politics. If they are city people, they've probably been on the streets. At eighteen the American male—out of self-interest if nothing else—begins to worry about war and peace; and the American female, about marriage and children. The American teenager has many other peepholes through which he may look at the way things seem to be. There are television and printed things and always, of course, automobiles. He undoubtedly has a lot to learn. On the other hand, it should not be assumed that his mind is a blank slate just waiting for some eager college to write on. It's a mind containing some very definite ideas at a time in life which is exploratory.

At the other end of the university experience adults between the ages of twenty and thirty emerge "educated."

Many have made the marriage commitment. Most have been compelled to choose careers. They have either exercised the franchise or are about to vote.

The college years are swept by tumultuous crosscurrents. They are a time for choosing—for making the basic decisions about the future even while reconsidering the beliefs, convictions, and habits accumulated through growing up at home.

It is a time of life loaded with potential for release—physical, spiritual, and intellectual. How can a learning community best accommodate this energy potential? How can this great youthful drive best be directed toward constructive and creative ends?

Most of our colleges shaped their answers to these questions in a preurban epoch—before television and automobiles; before World War II, Korea, and Vietnam; before the opportunity for higher education was expanded from an élite privilege to a popular expectation and right.

Most of our college campuses are still designed to be homes away from home, environmental cushions against the shock of social and intellectual dislocation, idealizations of the homes and communities from which the students come, rigged to stress a continuity in life styles and patterns. They are "homes" in which the morality the American middle class preaches is actually supposed to be practiced. They are communities planned to reassure the parents of the students that going to college will not challenge what the adults in power represent; and, apparently, to reassure the students that college life can be beautiful even if the higher learning at times can be rough.

The trouble with the home-away-from-home concept is that the models—unlike the realities—contain thousands of "children," and, instead of the conventional two parents, there is a phalanx of mothers and fathers: lines of deans, directors, and counselors whose main purpose is to lead the "children" through the intricacies and subtleties of collegiate family life. The idealized result is a kind of caricature of reality. "Home" becomes a welfare state—a community environment specially controlled for the conduct of the great experiment called "Education for Freedom."

The student-citizens are housed and fed by the central government. Their sex conduct is supposed to be carefully supervised. Their health is cared for through the state's health clinics. As they march into the classrooms, their names are checked off lists. In their pockets are special identification badges carrying certain welfare privileges. Formal self-government is officially encouraged, but the sovereignty of student government is rigorously limited by a superior authority which combines the power of the father with the power of the state. The students are encouraged to join and to lead, but most of the regulations of student life are directed toward a confirmation of the restrictive responsibilities of leadership, the recitation of the limits upon the exercise of leadership power. Students, taught in the classrooms that there is an indispensable relationship between self-government and the exercise of intelligence in political conduct, observe that on the campus the practice of politics apparently contaminates that delicate and precious flower— "the educational process."

Leisure time is carefully planned in the hopeful expectation that the children will not become bored and bothersome. There are the parties, dances, mixers, the grand and colorful sports circuses.

Of course, many students quickly learn how to beat the welfare state at its own game or manage somehow to stand aloof from those family activities in which participation is not required.

In the typical American college, the mean age in the student body is near twenty. In the large universities, the mean age is over twenty-one. Female legal majority in most of the states of the union is eighteen. A woman can get married without parental consent at that age. In most states, people can operate automobiles at sixteen or eighteen. We conscript American males for military service and send them away to fight our wars at the age of nineteen. During the college years, most of our students, simply by growing older, may purchase and consume liquor and tobacco, and may vote, incur debt, and undertake most of the rights and duties of full citizenship in this country.

Student freedom is the greatest threat to arbitrary academic administrative and faculty power. There is no more important dimension to the education of the college student than the experience of being free in the regulation of his personal life and with regard to the public affairs of his community. The special laws and government imposed on the younger citizens of the American campus may mislead parents into feeling better. But they do not contribute to the higher education of the American young.

The laboratory is an essential and indispensable part of science education. Millions of dollars are spent for the construction of science laboratories in which the students may experiment. In freedom education, the learning community is itself the essential laboratory. Until this fact is recognized by those who teach and administer in the universities, there will be more rather than less student unrest and discontent. And there should be. The students are potentially the most powerful spearhead for the reform of the academic community. For them, the most vital issues of the community's life are not salary schedules, rank and promotion, tenure, status, and prestige. For them, the overriding issue is the redistribution of power in the community in order to implement goals bearing upon the way they will live. The student unrest, whether expressed about Vietnam, civil rights, General Hershey, or Dow Chemical, is really about education.

Within the memory of most of us, the ideas of democracy

to which we Americans aspire have been viciously assaulted
from both political extremes—from the fascist right and
from the communist left. Today, perhaps more than ever
before, the assaults are mounted from the inside. The new
concentrations of power through science and technology,
the extraordinary concentration of people in the expanding
cities, and the complex and often mysterious bureaucracies
through which the power is organized in the hope of control
—these are not wholly American inventions. Under the um-
brella of a single nation-state, as these forces rain down upon
us, we Americans are compelled to live together in peace—
we Americans, who among ourselves are all the races of man;
we Americans, who among ourselves embody almost all of
the ethnic, national, and cultural traditions and heritages of
civilization. In a unique way, our domestic challenge is not
national, but international, and the American dilemma is
the workshop of a planetary situation. Foreign and domestic
policies flow and are locked together in our case—a fact I
hope we are beginning to understand better now as the
meaning of the Vietnam toll becomes more widely understood.

The great technological and bureaucratic events of our
time have aroused the passions, the anxieties, and the fears
of our people as well as their hopes. Thousands of us,
whether we like it or not, whether we intended to be or not,
find ourselves standing on the cutting edges of this nation's
life. We cannot, even if we wished to, sit behind closed
campus doors and drawn academic blinds wringing our
hands and hoping that our deep problems will somehow
magically disappear. We cannot hide or disguise what we
have inherited or what we are creating. We are in the open.
We are on the city streets, exposing and exposed. Our minds,
and the ways we organize what we do with them, are the
best weapons we have, however frail and imperfect they
may be.

The ghettoization of a person, a part of a city, a college, or the outlook of a nation presents a formidable intellectual and moral challenge. That's the challenge to education for freedom now.

We asked the administration if Stokely Carmichael could come to our campus as a speaker. (Over eighty percent of our students are black.) The response was that if Carmichael came there would be riots. They were telling us that the students weren't intelligent enough to listen to Carmichael without rioting. So we went to the students and asked them if they wanted to hear Carmichael. More than 4,500 signed petitions saying they'd like to hear him, so we brought him to the campus without the consent of the Administration. We felt that the collective voice of the students should be heard.

I was charged with "Gross Disrespect for University Officials." I was suspended along with 70 other students. The suspension was indefinite. But immediately after it was official—within a week—I was drafted.

I felt that the suspension and the draft denied me due process of law. I refused induction. I was brought to court and sentenced, and I'm out on appeal now.

—*Extract from a letter from a black student leader formerly in a university in the South, March 1968*

VIII

Something for Everybody Is Not Enough

First and last, cities are people—all else comes in between as links and tools of people—and people are psychological organisms conducting themselves in certain ways which determine the character and quality of their habitations. A slum is at first sight a physical condition. But in fact it is even more a state of mind. A farmhouse in the great open spaces can be as unkempt and disorderly as a cold-water tenement in a congested East Side. In the first instance it is people who make slums, not slums which make people. That comes later.

HORACE M. KALLEN[37]

OUR FORMAL educational systems have broken down at every level in the urban anti-cities. The result is a crisis in the operation of basic American principles.

One of the country's largest black communities is in Brooklyn. Almost a half million people, 90 percent black and most of the others Puerto Rican, live in Bedford-Stuyvesant. The community contains several beautiful parks, fine brownstone houses, and active church congregations. Many of the outstanding leaders it has produced take great pride in the community and continue to live there. Scores of civic organizations are at work in the community. There are major public-housing and poverty-program investments. There is

a growing cadre of intelligent and articulate parents directing attention upon the public-school system.

Bedford-Stuyvesant contains some of the worst housing in
the United States. Over half of its youth between the ages of
fifteen and nineteen are neither in school nor employed. The
community has a higher rate of juvenile delinquency than
Harlem—twice that for the city as a whole. In Bedford-
Stuyvesant universal public education means that the median
school year completed is 8.9. Less than one percent of its
people have gone to college. (Nationally over half of American high-school graduates enter college.)

A report of one agency working in Bedford-Stuyvesant
says that "for any young man to drop out from school is
equivalent to committing economic suicide."[38] But the
youngsters who stick with the schools in this community
commit themselves to something not much better. Over 80
percent of those who do stick leave high school with nonacademic diplomas which generally bar college admission.
The commercial and vocational certificates they earn hap-
hazardly prepare them for jobs rapidly being eradicated by
technology. Even then, many are led toward work which
requires membership in unions that discriminate.

There were serious riots in Bedford-Stuyvesant in the
summer of 1964. F.B.I. reports following those riots concluded that "the majority of the participants were teenagers,
most of whom were unemployed high-school dropouts with
nothing better to do."[39] There has been violence in the streets
of this community every summer since.

Lower education is a public monopoly in Bedford-Stuyvesant. The few private competing systems are small, church-
based, and in continuous financial trouble.

By the standards of all higher-education systems, public
and private, the products of the public schools serving
Bedford-Stuyvesant are "deficient." They do not perform
well according to the established standards. But these stand-

ards have a direct bearing upon how these young people perform; they tend to perpetuate rather than confront the problem of the community.

The teacher-education programs in the universities feeding personnel into this community's schools are simply inadequate. The middle-class products of these programs do not have the vaguest understanding of life in the anti-city. They are admitted to the university programs largely because they are middle class, and their educational experience points them even more directly toward middle-class professional and community life. They are prepared to serve middle-class school children, to the extent that they are prepared at all.

The appearance of the white middle-class teacher in the black anti-city classroom is too often like the appearance of the colonial civil servant in some remote outpost of the empire. The "educational opportunity" such a teacher represents is imperialistic. Black parents and often the children greet this teacher with suspicion and hostility. More often than not, the teacher's response is fear—fear of the alien work environment in which the *teacher* is the minority, fear of professional challenges for which the teacher is unprepared. The easiest way to accommodate such fear is in a further deprecation, not of self, but of the situation—especially of the children, who are the most immediate elements in the situation. The act of teaching becomes rigged to service the "deficiencies" of these children, not to explore and exploit their human potential.

The teacher is caught in the arbitrary and artificial organization of the formal-educational systems—an organization which encourages the bureaucracies monopolizing each part to blame the others for its own failures. Planning and operational authority is divided between "lower" and "higher" systems, spreading a bureaucratic grease over responsibility, making it impossibly slippery and difficult to keep in hand.

Administrative barriers erected between elementary and secondary at the lower level, and between undergraduate, graduate, and professional at the higher, compartmentalize thought and confound the implementation of new educational programs.

The lower systems point toward the failure of the teacher training centers in the universities. The universities point toward the "deficient" products of the lower systems—students about whom the universities can do nothing because they simply are not admissible. In the abstract, everyone agrees that failure in any one part is connected to failures in the others. Operationally, each part jealously guards its separate powers.

The "critical" educational thresholds get pushed further and further down the age scale. To get the students in condition for college admissibility, the high schools undergo major reform. Reform at the high-school level depends upon revision of the elementary programs. Kindergarten is too late, thus Head Start. Head Start is not enough—the life of the infant from six months on is crucial. Each part of the formal-educational system brilliantly exposes breakdowns in sectors beyond its jurisdiction.

Everyone who comes to a formal-educational system, regardless of his prior experience—*because* of his prior experience—presents a special "problem" to that system. The very "gifted" present a very difficult problem. The going system was not especially designed to accommodate them. The typical middle-class collegian presents an extraordinary educational "problem." He may fit into the going system too comfortably. The existence of difficult educational problems is not special. The incapacity of the formal-educational systems to come to grips with the "problems" of the anti-city youth *is* special. What these young people represent is alien to the expectations and to the main interests of the going systems. In principle, the going systems cannot reject the "outsiders." In principle, they must aim to get everybody "in." But, in practice, they do reject the outsiders because they don't conform.

There are 30 institutions of higher education in New York City on 41 different campuses. In the fall of 1967 they enrolled almost 300,000 students—more than enrolled in the universities of any single country of Western Europe. Almost one out of four of New York City's citizens is black or Puerto Rican. About four or five percent of the full-time university enrollments in the city come from these groups.

In the private schools, the average annual tuition fees are equal to a little more than half of the average annual family income in Bedford-Stuyvesant. Through their scholarship programs and with federal assistance, these schools have enrolled proportionately more black students in their regular four-year college programs than the free-tuition public system. There is an inverse relationship, however, between the reputed "quality" of the recipient institutions and their black and Puerto Rican enrollments. The range is from one to ten percent—the "better" the school, the lower the percentage. On all of these campuses there is very little social or political intercourse between black and white. Separatist Afro-American student clubs thrive. The occasions for power confrontations multiply on all of the "integrated" model campuses.

Full-time black enrollments in the four-year units of the free-tuition public university in New York average a little more than three percent. On the campus located in Harlem, the figure is a bit over four percent, and on the one in Brooklyn closest to Bedford-Stuyvesant, it was 2.5 percent of the full-time students in the fall of 1967.

Students currently not "qualified" for full-time status in the day programs of the public-university system may enroll as part-time, nonmatriculated students at night. Black enrollments in this status are comparatively higher. But the students at night pay tuition for the privilege of a second-class academic citizenship, and it is not clear how many emerge from this category into the mainstream that gets the union card, the degree. In a very literal sense, the part-time, non-degree night students contribute financially to the support of the education of the essentially middle-class, full-time "qualified" day students in the free-tuition public-university system of New York.*

The lower-school systems of our great cities are on the frontlines of social and political upheaval. The colleges and universities are still shoring up their defenses. To the salient educational crisis of our time, their response is loud and clear: a firm reassertion of the traditional ways of doing business. Even the "special" search-and-discovery scholarship programs all assume that the search will lead to the discovery of "underprivileged" youth, who, subjected to minor patch-up jobs, can be made to "fit" into the traditional system. The traditional admission criteria, the old ways of teaching, the rigid conceptions of what knowledge is relevant, and the inflexibility in the presentation of that knowledge—all are assumed "right." What is presumed wrong is the incapacity of the "underprivileged" to qualify and/or the social ills which result in that incapacity. Regarding the former, the Establishments are prepared to make modest exceptions pursuant to the patch-up jobs. About the latter, direct attacks on the social ills are viewed as beyond the academic jurisdiction.

The two-year colleges in the great cities of the country are especially designed to bridge the gap between the traditionally "right" criteria of the full-blown four-year colleges and the higher-educational needs of the young people who

* The record of accommodation and service for minority groups in the State University of New York—a complex even larger than the free-tuition system in the City of New York—is equally unimpressive. There is evidence that the tax-supported state system is performing behind the private colleges and universities in New York in the admission of black and Puerto Rican students.

do not measure up to those criteria—of the academically "underprivileged" and the "culturally deprived." In many places, these institutions are called "junior colleges." In New York City, they are known as "community colleges." While they have turned out in almost every respect to be "junior," they seldom are related effectively to the communities in which they happen to be located.

These colleges should be on the frontline of higher-educational innovation in the United States. They are supposed to be addressed to the vital connection between advanced education and economic survival. They are meant to open up higher-educational opportunity to more people, and thus they should be closer to the people they serve, should invent new ways to achieve that closeness and to serve those young adults about whom the established four-year colleges are most suspect and wary. But they must live with the limitations built into them for very special purposes. They were not meant to be an innovative challenge to the Establishment. They were meant to be a shield to keep safe those values which the established colleges and universities revere most.

In the order of higher education, the two-year colleges have low status and low prestige. The degrees they produce have low value on the job and in the academic marketplaces. They are limited to two years in order to maintain the senior system's monopoly over the more important degrees and curricular provinces upon which the higher degrees depend. This jurisdictional limitation seriously restricts the professional and vocational goals the two-year institution can perfect. These colleges are seldom bases for high prestige research. The high-status liberal arts rarely occupy a prominent place in their curricula. Aspirations for their students are meant to be pegged—not just academically, but socially and economically. They produce *sub, semi,* and *para* professionals. Rubrics such as "technology" and "engineering" dominate their academic programs. These categories may encompass anything from training secretaries, automobile mechanics, and computer operators to television repairmen, nurses' assistants, and firemen. These are all honorable callings. Many require post-high-school education. But these are not the professions, the classes of decision making and power toward which a higher education in the U.S. is generally thought to lead.

The two-year colleges often offer liberal-arts programs which permit transfer into a senior-college system. But the senior system regards these programs as pale versions of its own, bargain-basement pathways into the main-floor operations of academe. The brevity of the two-year terms does not allow for much mind changing by students who are uncertain about their professional goals at the point of entry. In the four-year colleges, the students may still defer a career choice until the end of the first year and often into the second or third—the growing pressures of the graduate and professional schools notwithstanding. But in the vocationally oriented two-year college, a choice must be made early in the game, and that choice, usually leading to the study of a specialized vocation, precludes engagement in a broad-gauged curriculum from which there may be future educational or career mobility.

Given the limitations of their resources and the values honored by the larger system of which they are a part, the two-year colleges do a relatively good job. But they were created to be filters and safety valves—inventions to keep the established, conventional colleges from being overwhelmed by numbers and watered-down by those who do not conform to the prevailing quality standards. They were meant to create the impression of "college" at a level close to the new cadres wanting "in." But they have become tails on the kites of the old traditions rather than the pioneers of new ones.

"Success" for the teachers and the administrators in the two-year colleges generally means one thing: getting out and "up" into the four-year system.

In almost every respect the junior colleges result in the segregation of values and of people. They are often staffed by teachers and administrators who would rather be working in the more highly rewarding four-year colleges or universities. They are attended by students who would rather be in the four-year colleges but can't get in at the freshman level. They segregate by economic class, social status, and life aspiration because of the limited objectives they frame for their students. They segregate within the Establishment's terms. But worst of all, they segregate under conditions where the segregated feel no sense of possessiveness or control.*

The spectacular growth of the two-year colleges under public auspices throughout the United States reveals the higher-educational system's fundamental response to the extraordinary educational challenge we now face. The master plans for the great public-university systems in populous states such as California and New York declare the intention to provide something for everybody, but to make the provision in such a manner so as not to disturb the status quo of academic value. To each his own, at his own level, in his own milieu. The stratifications of American society are honored in the stratifications of the unfolding new educational plans. This is a politically pragmatic response to the challenge. It accepts the shortcomings of the lower systems and perpetuates them, projects them into the future lives of the people who have been damaged. It permits the higher-educational system to do something at a time when the

---

* In New York City, the community-college system enrolls about forty percent of the total number of students in all branches of the public, free-tuition university. About one-fourth of the full- and part-time enrollment is black and Puerto Rican.

people will not allow it to do nothing. It defends the bastions of tradition, keeping the loci of decision making in the heartland of the established system. It results in the enlargement of the power of the university without disturbing its ancient prejudices.

In this manner, two almost completely separate but parallel higher-educational systems may be created under one monopolistic management. One system is prestige-bound, shored up by arbitrarily rigged admission criteria, dominated by faculties reluctant to change habits developed in the distant past, led by power-conscious bureaucrats, and servicing the white middle class of the city. The other is without prestige, but with a mission, directed toward the poor and the lower levels of the middle class, and led by a professional cadre which is ambivalent about the mission because of its enchantment with the values of the senior system.

This political response of the higher-educational system reflects accurately the deep trouble our country is in right now. Variations on old themes simply will not do. The issue in the country *is* stratification. The issue in higher education *is* the old academic prejudices. Something for everybody is not enough, especially if the "something" is the further institutionalization of what is not working well. In Bedford-Stuyvesant more and more professionals, fearfully traveling into the community each day to work, are being paid higher and higher middle-class incomes as employees of educational institutions which are not working well. In great cities like New York, more and more people are being paid at higher and higher levels in the universities which have less and less to say to the young people of Bedford-Stuyvesant.

Social-security systems may be extended to enable less affluent older Americans to die in greater peace. The organization of the public dole may be perfected to permit the unemployable middle-aged to survive more peacefully with greater self-respect. Through the welter of educational experiments underway, new ways may yet be discovered to create for the very young and for those yet to be born new reasons for hope. But for the generation of young adults most badly bruised by the past failures of the lower-educational system, most quickly fired by the spirit of the new freedom movement, and most brutally frustrated in their efforts to express that spirit, what does America promise? They are too old to be turned back. They are too young to die in peace. Given the conditions under which they now face their future, they would be something less than good Americans if they settled for mere peaceful survival.

We make a serious mistake with this generation if we assume that jobs—of any kind at any price—are enough. Many of them are now in training programs being prepared for jobs which, if they exist after they are trained, will pay little more than the subsidies being paid to them while they are in the programs. Some of these young people, facing realistically the assumptions our society is making about their potential, are moving from one job-training program to another without the slightest intention of being trapped by any one of the low-status, low-paying jobs at the end of the training road. For many Americans, the job-training programs have led to a new career category—job training.

Having come with too little too late to the slums which produced them, our country has failed to provide the lower educational resources through which many of our young black Americans in the cities may realize their potential. Having allowed them to grow up under these conditions, we have failed to provide adult-learning institutions effectively addressed to the backwash of racism and slavery. How comforting it would be to a well-intentioned (and frightened) America, beckoning these young adults to enter the mainstream, if the vehicle for mainstream entry was simply the preparation of people who have had inadequate lower education for jobs which require no significant higher education.

But those who seek comfort in this simple economic analysis of our plight utterly misunderstand what is going on in the minds of young black adults—or in the minds of many young white ones, for that matter.

No educational effort will succeed with the young people in Bedford-Stuyvesant unless it carefully accommodates their intense search for the meaning of themselves. American society has made being black one of the primary, if not the most primary, element of self-identification for these people.

In our zeal to identify and condemn the horrible slums in which so many of the black people in our cities live, we often dishonor and degrade the pride many citizens feel for the communities in which they live. Bedford-Stuyvesant is not one, monolithic, unrelieved slum. Nor do many of the young adults living there feel particularly privileged or grateful for being paid, through one public program or another, to keep off the streets of the place where they live. Outsiders who refer to a place like Bedford-Stuyvesant as a "ghetto" assault many perfectly legitimate sources of community pride and strength. Our great cities are mosaics of ethnic, cultural, religious, and economic enclaves. Urban life in America breathes people in and out of *voluntary* "ghettos," breathes them in and out of the "integrated" centers where a common national discourse—economic, political, and cultural—is transacted. The attack upon the un-American, *involuntary* ghetto must not slip into a kind of condescension through which the white majority arbitrarily insists upon the conformity of the black minority in the name of some liberal notion of "integration."

Most of the urban colleges and universities either approach a community like Bedford-Stuyvesant—the people in it—with condescension, or conduct themselves as if such communities do not exist, as if the young adults who live there do not exist. They either reach out for a chosen few, on their terms, of course; or invoke splendid isolation. An institution for higher education addressed to the youth of Bedford-Stuyvesant must encourage its students to take pride in and connect to that community.

What white and middle-class America means by "freedom" is too often words, words, words for the young Americans living in the black urban communities. They have had little opportunity to possess and manage valuable things, to experience the responsibility of legitimate power, to be a part of groups or institutions through which effective and meaningful decision making takes place. They know the harsh meaning of the involuntary ghetto; but they know too little about what it means to *breathe* in the pattern of American urban life. They have grown up holding their breath until they are about ready to burst. For them, what white and middle-class American means by "freedom" is too often translated into meaningless, restrictive devices—into time clocks, forms and applications, tyrannical teachers presiding over jail-like classrooms. (The streets are "free.")

An essential part of educational planning for a Bedford-Stuyvesant must consist of constructing new contexts through which freedom, and the relationship of knowledge to being free, can be experienced. These new contexts must have a credibility and a sophistication far beyond the stilted and artificial environments so carefully constructed in many of our colleges and universities. They must extend to the realities of community life, to the places where the important work of the city is done, to the key events which relate the individual to the national and international affairs which shape his destiny.

A chance for the identification of self, the cultivation of a pride in and a sense of responsibility toward community, and enlarged opportunities for making the connections between freedom and learning—these are the only premises upon which the education of the young adults in the urban black communities can be built.

The imperfect implementation of these premises is the main generator of student unrest on campuses everywhere in the United States. The growing educational demands of American collegians who are already "in" coincide with the imperative requisites of an educational program for the youth of Bedford-Stuyvesant who are still searching for ways "in." On the educational front, as on so many other salient fronts in the United States, the black people are the cutting edges for the reform of our society. They, who have been the most abused by the realities of American life, shout loudest now in behalf of its promise.

My grandfather was a very wise man. He worked ten acres for a white man in Mississippi. He used to say, "Don't hate a man because of his color." I guess he thought it was okay to hate for the right reasons.

I've been around three riots. I've seen these cats burning and looting. But not me. What's the point of tearing down your own neighborhood? It reminds me of the army. There were so many Negro sergeants from the South. They were really rough with us black guys. Pin some stripes on those guys, and man—do they integrate! I hated some of those sergeants.

When they tell me to integrate, they're saying: "Cool it." I'm not so sure. Not on Whitey's terms. Maybe after I'm equipped. I don't want their love. One way or another they're going to respect me. Then maybe *they'll* be ready to integrate!

   —*From a conversation with a Vietnam veteran,*
             April 1968

IX

Toward Renewal

What we have to learn to do, we learn by doing.

ARISTOTLE

To LEARN, people have to want to learn. Good intentions, new buildings, and tried and true methodologies and curricula have been imported into the ghettos, and failed. The ultimate test of any combination of teachers, books, buildings, equipment, administrative structures, and curricular schemes is whether they move people to *act,* influence their *conduct* in behalf of learning. People who want to learn, learn. An educational bureaucracy can help or hinder the process, but it can't stop it. It can, however, be a decisive force in creating a desire to learn and an environment for learning.

Where are we to look for the wellsprings of motivation?

Every educational system takes a special view of knowledge. It embodies a selection of what seems most important and relevant to those empowered to select at a particular time and place. The selection is always presented in forms and styles harmonious with the value judgments made about the content. It is easy to understand why the British, during the Empire, imposed their educational and university systems upon the colonials and why, after independence, the Nigerians, the Indians, and many of the others immediately

felt the need for new invention and major educational reform. In our acceptance, rejection, additions to, and refine-
ments of what we took from the British, German, French,
and Italian universities, we Americans have written a history
of our own culture and translated it into institutional forms.
Every educational system embodies and projects the values
of the society it serves, and assumes that those values will
motivate people, move them to act, and influence their conduct in certain ways in the communities in which they live.

As measured by the American values, the ghetto is a de-
cayed community. It does not react in the usual ways to the
usual inducements. What is presented as education there
does not evoke the expected responses. So much of it lacks
relevance in the experience of the people living there. The
young are not moved by what we expect to move them, nor
are their parents.

A parallel puzzlement has cropped up on the campuses
of our strongest colleges and universities serving the most
carefully screened, the élite of the nation's youth. Raised in
the cities and suburbs, exposed in the middle-class way to
the technological success, moved around earlier in a greater
variety of life experiences, and encouraged while young to
think about the worst of the problems in the "adult" world,
the cream of the crop is reacting with less and less enthusiasm to the ways of the established educational system.
More and more of these students no longer "fit" comfortably
into the system. To put it another way: The system no longer
fits adequately the aspirations and the life experiences of
these students.

The college campus is a decaying community. The "community of scholars" is brittle and artificial. It has declined in
a territorial and in an institutional sense. There are associations of specialists which transcend institutional and geographic limitations, held together by common interests in
a discipline and by the problems arising out of it. But within

the campus, there is a massive disengagement of the teachers from each other and from the students. Research, reduced teaching loads, a mechanical processing system, and the material rewards of professional status dominate whatever common discourse is left. The institutional setting in which this discourse occurs is now relatively irrelevant.

The urban "campus community" is sterile and make-believe. At best, it is like a nine-to-five place of work—like an office or a store. Student government is tokenism. Faculty government is increasingly unionism. Residence halls are hotels. The conduct of management, not the conduct of learning, is the issue of the day.

The university's relationship to the territorial-political community in which it is located is restive and uneasy. Though it may be the most important economic and physical component in its neighborhood, the university invariably is the most conservative and aloof resident thereof.

Powerlessness is at the core of the decay of the ghetto community. The calcification of power systems and the insensitive and irresponsible use of great power have undermined the campus community. In both cases, a terrible gap has appeared between the values professed and the instrumentalities produced for the realization of those values. In both cases, what the prevailing systems ask the people to do seems less and less relevant to their life experience and aspirations. In both cases, the impact of technology and new knowledge upon American values has resulted in institutional forms and bureaucratic control systems which further subvert the values and frustrate the aspirations of our people.

New institutional forms and ways of accommodating the educational aspirations of our people must be invented to bridge this dangerous gap in American life.

The urban-suburban centers where most of our people now live and work are the key staging grounds for the renewal effort. These centers are direct coefficients of the technological success and the new knowledge. The future of our higher-educational institutions is irrevocably bound to them. But the future quality and tone of the urban centers hinge in many ways on how the issues raised by our black people are resolved. A great many chips have been placed on education for the successful resolution of these issues. The two urban communities reflecting the strongest anti-city tendencies—the ghetto and the campus—share a rendezvous with a common destiny.

Very few of the many new colleges and universities being built have chosen the ghetto for a home or the educational problems of these communities as a central challenge. As the expanding slums and the crises in values have encroached upon the established campuses and the traditional academic programs, the institutions have either built their walls higher or fled. But there are fewer and fewer "safe" places in which to locate an urban campus, and there are fewer and fewer "safer" versions of their responsibilities which the colleges and universities can persuade the American people to accept. *A moment of truth and a time of great risk have arrived for the American academics.**

---

* "The question may well be asked how and in what ways . . . the physical features of a college campus, including the neighborhood in which it is placed, help or hinder the stated function and educational program of that institution?

". . . Physical surroundings . . . exercise an obvious and powerful influence on the community of persons who live and work in them. Love of books and art, good talk, of satisfying work with friends and colleagues; the knowledge of and sense of belonging to the great world beyond political, national, racial or religious divisions; personal dignity; the suggestions, through beauty, order, cleanliness and grace, of what is possible and noble in the development of human existence—all these do not come about automatically through classroom work alone, and cannot come about for students in an environment which is as crowded, hectic and oppressive as, for example, the City's subways themselves.

". . . A new college is spirit and morale. . . . A tired and decaying neighborhood, or old and shabby rented facilities, kill an eager and fresh spirit very quickly. . . . Neighborhood distractions, encroachments, in-

Such moments have faced us before. In Jefferson's time, the European university models had to be transformed into institutions capable of producing a new leadership for a society based on startlingly new political premises. A direct line was drawn between formal education and the capacity for self-government. To draw this line, the university had to be moved further off its religious onto a secular base. New classes and new knowledge had to be admitted.

In the midst of civil war and in the growing backwash of industrialization, a new transformation occurred in the mid-nineteenth century. A direct line was drawn between formal education and the equalization of economic condition and social status. To draw this line, the land-grant institution had to be invented. Here again new classes and new knowledge had to be admitted.

Now new and complicated lines must be drawn connecting the technological success and the urban way of life to the central values of American society. One of the first places in which these lines must be drawn is in the center of the nation's most troubled areas—in the urban communities

conveniences, resentments, can poison and deaden that atmosphere. . . . Approaches to a modern urban campus through avenues of physical decay and moral blight take their toll of high purpose and firm resolve. Vistas of ugly and depressing campus surroundings take their toll in good morale.

"A college need not be in a ghetto to know that ghettos exist. And being in a ghetto will not in itself produce a curriculum or educational ideal which touches that ghetto, as shown by a CUNY college which has been called 'an island in Harlem' and by a major private university whose relationship with its neighborhood is simply one of warfare. . . .

"A university in the first instance is not a political, social, or economic response to particular community problems of a given time and place.

"(Campus space requirements for the new college have been established as follows: instructional, 2,800,000 square feet; student and faculty residential, 690,000 square feet; parking, 1,500,000 square feet. Fifty-five million dollars has been specified in the University's Master Plan for land acquisition and building construction.)" [Excerpts from the *Report of the Committee on Campus Planning and Development of the Board of Higher Education,* York College of the City University of New York, Site Selection Study, Part I, January 17, 1968.]

where most of our black people live. To draw the lines, our colleges and universities must test some principles which challenge their most revered traditions.

FIRST: The old demarcation line separating the jurisdiction of the higher-educational system from the lower makes less and less educational sense. Impressive failures in each sector create a new kind of interdependence between them. A reasonable accommodation of the varying educational growth rates of real people (as distinguished from the artificial categorizations of people with which the systems like to deal) is almost precluded by the present division of bureaucratic, fiscal, planning, and program power between the two levels—between high school and what went before, and college and what follows.

It has long been recognized that the last one, two, or three years in many of our high schools are an utter waste of time for many of those students labeled "bright" by the system's own standards. (Most of these years are certainly a waste of time in the ghettos.) For some students, the first, second, or third years of college are repetitive and wasteful. A few colleges have dipped down into the secondary schools with early-admission programs. Some high schools and colleges have tried to patch up these "misfit" situations with special "enrichment" or "honors" programs. But these operations only nibble at the larger problem, which pertains not only to the more "gifted," but to young people of an almost infinite variety of talents and capacities. The larger problem is the way we have permitted rigid managerial systems, false notions about prestige and status, and arbitrary jurisdictional barriers to come between the potential of young people and the educational resources and talents best able to release that potential.

Admission into the higher system (with all of the practical consequences that follow) especially depends upon reading, verbal, and mathematical skills. The basic educational preparation in these areas is the responsibility of the lower system. The higher system is ill-equipped to get at the potential of people which may be reflected through talents other than proficiency in these skills. It is disinclined to honor the meaning of the other talents. Performance in higher-educational programs largely depends upon the student's verbal and mathematical proficiencies. A student with abilities which he cannot express in these ways is rejected. In his case, the lower system has failed and the higher system is closed. The failure of the lower system may have its roots in any number of causes, but the most common sources of the problem are in the family and community environment and in the incapacity of the lower school. The relationship of adults to the child in the home and in the community presents a sophisticated educational challenge which the lower system is badly prepared to face and the higher largely ignores.

The young person at fourteen, fifteen or sixteen who is "deficient" in verbal and mathematical performance is nobody's responsibility. The lower system has written him off; the higher system won't touch him. His future in the American economy is dead-ended. He falls between the jurisdictional boards of the two failing educational systems, and for all practical purposes his formal education is over. He has failed.

The impact of technology and new knowledge upon the middle- and higher-income-level jobs in our society has had a tremendous influence within our educational systems. The more specialized and demanding the job calling, the deeper the preparation for that calling reaches into the educational systems. The graduate and professional schools seriously delimit the range of undergraduate educational choice. The undergraduate colleges impose their requirements upon the secondary schools. Frequently, an educational decision is forced upon first- or second-year high-school students, people at the ages of fourteen or fifteen, which circumscribes almost irrevocably their future career or professional options. Informally, the lower system often makes conclusive judgments about the future economic survival capacity of its students much earlier in the game. Young people who fall behind in reading and verbal skills at the second-, third- or fourth-grade levels are often pegged by the system, and in effect "written off" insofar as future mobility is concerned. Judgments are made about the college admissibility of these young children before they are out of grade school. Is it any wonder that so many of them subsequently "drop out." They may be acting wisely by getting out. What they lose "educationally" they may gain in mental health.

These profoundly important economic decisions are made about people within the terms of one system, in anticipation of the terms of another. The result is a horrendous mismatch of talent and career opportunity, and the setting of the stage for the advanced miseducation of many people in an area of their lives where it really hurts—the vocations from which they will derive income for the rest of their lives.

The universities monopolizing the education of those who aim to teach in the lower schools have become inexcusably detached and remote from the realities of the classrooms. The administrators of the lower-school monopolies, whose directives establish the conditions under which people can teach, are often out of touch with what the university people now think a higher education should be, or with what they think the bill of fare for a well-educated teacher ought to be. Job-promotion requirements imposed by the lower systems are increasingly out of step with the best thought about what postgraduate education ought to be. But the best thought about that is often completely irrelevant to the realities of being a teacher. University-level research in the field of education is poorly communicated to and in the lower systems, and even more poorly translated into actual programs. But practical wisdom frequently achieved through the classroom too rarely penetrates the curricula of the teacher-training centers.

The separate and autonomous authorities of the lower- and the higher-educational systems must be replaced formally by a shared responsibility in at least three areas to begin with: the education of teachers, the education of the adults whose children are in the lower schools, and the education of young people from the ages of fourteen or fifteen up.

The mobilization of the resources of the two systems must far more accurately respond to that period in the educational process when the economic, political, social, and cultural demands of the postschool, adult world begin to take hold and influence deeply the formal education and the day-to-day lives of young people. This period is no longer at seventeen or eighteen years of age in our society, especially in the black urban communities. It more closely corresponds to the realities of the biological development of the human being, to the significant physical, psychological, and cultural events which begin to occur when a person crosses the line from childhood to adolescence and which happen with increasing rapidity throughout the time of the teens into young adulthood. It is during this period that the value of money, experimentation with sex, the transfer of loyalty to the peer group, the challenge to adult authority and adult systems, and the bruising impact of the adult world all enter and often take over the lives of the young people, often with devastating consequences. And it is during this period that the existing systems close rather than open the doors to formal-educational opportunity; conclude rather than begin the decisions regarding the future; contract rather than expand the relationships between the educational experience and the compelling economic, political, and social realities of the larger environment.

The planning and implementation of "advanced education" for the youth of the black urban communities should be the collaborative responsibility of the existing lower and higher systems throughout that stage now called "high school." Formal college education for these people should begin not later than at the age of sixteen. The repair of whatever educational damage American society and the lower system have done to these young people requires the engagement of the best resources of the lower and higher systems, and they must work together to turn around what has become an unforgivably dreadful situation. The great potential of a strategic generation of black Americans cannot be written off. The young black victims of our prejudice and incompetence are not going to go away. They will go where we make it possible for them to go. If we rig our educational systems so that they must go into the streets, we will find them in the streets.

SECOND: The strategic institutional power of the university in a broad range of the important affairs of the community in which it is located must be more directly responsive to the authority, management, will, and needs of that community. More and more people and institutions in the community are directly affected by the expanding monopoly powers of the university. But very few devices have been created to enable those who are affected by this power to control it, or even hold it responsible and accountable.

The more anti- or non-urban the community in which the university is located, the more impressive and far-reaching the institution's powers. Indiana University is decisive in the quality, tone, and material well-being of its town, Bloomington. Cornell is decisive in Ithaca. Even in large cities where but one major university operates, or in urban areas where a university dominates a substantial neighborhood, the power of the institution is crucial. Remove Indiana from Bloomington or Cornell from Ithaca or Wayne State from Detroit, and the community which remains will be seriously, if not hopelessly, impoverished economically, culturally, and in every other way.

An academic institution purposely located in the black urban community, designed especially to serve that community, is bound to have a tremendous regenerative power in its neighborhood. Its presence will affect the economy as well as the cultural and political life of the people. It may have a profound effect upon lower education in the community. Through its adult and community educational efforts, it may reach out to the strategic adult decision-making centers. By the choice of its physical location, it can influence the renewal of neighborhoods. Through the professional classes it attracts to the community, it may have an impact upon housing and commercial patterns.

Under these circumstances, the trustees of the college or the university—the people responsible for its properties, the deployment of its wealth, the delineation of its educational purposes and thrusts—must be chosen from among the people living or with a vested interest in the community it serves.

We claim that our academic institutions educate people for freedom in this country. The institutions which claim this mission cannot themselves be exempt from the operation of freedom principles. If we do not create institutions in the black urban communities which are free, which provide practical freedom experiences, then we cannot expect these communities to be motivated by, to honor and respect those values this nation professes to respect and honor.

The rejuvenation of the decaying urban communities in this country requires a substantial transfer of power from white to black, from established and traditional centers to innovative and new ones. This transfer must engage and involve the deployment of our best and most sophisticated intellectual, technical, and administrative talents. The confrontation between the experts and the people in the context of a power transfer is the most important event in the rejuvenation of the black urban communities. Indeed, it may very well be the most important event in the redefinition of the American experiment. The event must be enacted democratically. The higher-educational institution in the city, because of its purposes, powers, and responsibilities, must be the pioneer of this event, the explorer of this confrontation.

THIRD: The urban landscape and the topography of new knowledge invite innovation in the construction of new centers for learning in the city.

The superblock campus is a physical representation of monopoly—insular, monolithic, and exclusive. It operates like a fortress rather than in terms of a series of stations and connecting life channels throughout a community. It assumes that people will come to it, disarmed, on its terms, rather than that it should go to the people prepared to confront the terms of their lives. It centralizes buildings, activities, and power for the purpose of its own defense, rather than disperses and diffuses its resources in order to equip the people with the educational powers to defend themselves.

The various units of the new college should be built in relation to the variety of relevant resources the urban community possesses and on a scale that corresponds to the way the community is or hopes to be. The monumentality of the academic buildings should derive from their relevance to the tasks of education in a living community, not merely from their looks or size. They should encourage an enlarged flow of more qualitative neighborhood life. They should not choke off streets, preempt vital territory, distort the flow of human traffic, and artificially and arbitrarily reorder community activity. The academic buildings should represent a process, not a conclusion; streams in motion, not a dead sea; change, not status.

Consequently, in the location and design of the college buildings, questions must be asked about the relationship between the educational activities which will go on in them and the ongoing significance of existing parks, centers of commerce and industry, schools, churches, medical centers, libraries, streets of residence, transportation flows, and the places where civic and governmental affairs are conducted. How may the new academic buildings and the activities planned for them contribute to and enhance the purposes of the existing community resources and agencies? How may the strength of the community's life best be supportive of the higher-educational function? How may existing buildings in the community, abandoned and derelict, best be revitalized and converted to productive educational service?

The residence-hall barracks or hotel is an unnatural way for students to live in the urban community. It distorts human relationships. It discourages people from doing at home what they would normally do at home. The students should live in buildings on streets where the people of the community and their teachers live. They should share with them the experience of those streets and the life in them. Indeed, some educational functions may best be performed in buildings which include residential, commercial, and other nonacademic components. To the extent that the new college must build residences for transient students and teachers, it should build them in the style and dimension best corresponding to the residential aspirations of the people in the community where it builds. As for the others, the college itself should be so enmeshed and intertwined with the architecture and life of its community that living at home is at once natural, desirable, and like living "on campus."

The best physical climate for learning is one that is at ease with its natural surrounding, one that can draw inspiration from its environment and being at ease with it, can, reciprocally, inspire its environment. In building the urban college, the central educational purpose should be to infuse life into learning and learning into life. The ideal "campus" for the university in the city is the city—what it is and what its people hope it will become.

Fourth: People work in the places of learning, and

people learn in the places of working. Each experience is unique, but scholarly preaching remote from practice tends to be as sterile as practice becomes when it is detached from the infusion of ideas. The best education is never purely contemplative any more than the best job performance is unadulterated action. Learning in any field at any time involves experimentation, or should. Trial and error is implicit in learning. Ideas have to be tried on through action. The best learning process is a special pattern of repose and action, of thinking and doing. The pattern must specially fit the meeting between a particular student and a given subject matter.

At the times when our educational systems compel most young people to decide whether they will be lawyers, doctors, or Indian chiefs for the rest of their lives, most are utterly ignorant of what it actually is to be a lawyer, doctor, or Indian chief. If this is true of white middle-class youth (which it is), it is even more true of the youth of the black urban communities where the law does not represent justice, but trouble; where medicine is equated with the degrading chaos of the public-health clinic waiting room or the vagaries of the corner drugstore; and where Indians may stand for that occasion when the American nation last committed genocide upon a people.

The black youth of our time know something about what it is to be a post-office clerk, a nurses' aide, a bus driver, an automobile mechanic, a "hustler," a sales clerk, a domestic, a janitor, a secretary, or unemployed. But the important decision-making posts in our society to which they aspire— about which we, the majority, now talk as if we hope they will aspire—for most represent centers of mystery and oppression, remote, ominous, and unattainable.

To get action in the urban black communities now, it is not enough to promise pie in the sky. Experience has taught the people living there that the future is remote and unreal and, at the very least, unreliable. What counts necessarily is *now*. The rigors of a learning discipline cannot be imposed successfully upon people on the basis of vague and poorly understood future payoffs. We have created a society here in which the powerless, intentionally kept that way for a long time, do not have the vaguest experience with what it means to be powerful. Yet the powerful expect them, the powerless, to be motivated and guided most by what the powerful know and the powerless don't. This attitude and expectation is the essence of the imperialism imposed by the majority upon their black fellow citizens. Having denied to them the chance to be American, we are now upset with them for their failure to act as we think we act—to act in keeping with the values we preach but have put into practice so imperfectly in their case.

The new urban college, paced by a 12 months a year, six days a week urban calendar, should insure to every student part-time employment in an internship position intimately connected to his declared professional educational goal and/or academic subject of greatest interest at the point of admission. He should work in such an internship throughout his collegiate career.

Students who aim to be teachers should be interns in classrooms from the day they enter college until they earn their degrees. People who aspire to managerial, administrative, and executive positions in industry, government, cultural, medical, and other institutions should be associated in learning relationships with people who actually perform in such positions throughout the duration of their college experience. Pre-law students should alternate annually in internships as assistants to judges practicing in the civil and criminal court systems of the city, and as aides in the offices of lawyers.

The places where these kinds of professional and decision-making work are done must be regarded as classrooms or laboratories of the college in the same sense that study places in the academic buildings are. The people who directly supervise and guide the students in their internship performance should enjoy faculty status in the same way that others teaching in the college enjoy such status. They should be regarded as working members of the faculty, sharing in the overall guidance of the student and in the design of curricula.

For industry, government, and the wide range of city institutions now seeking ways to use their multifaceted resources in the effort to gain full citizenship for the black people and their communities, the internship program of the new college provides a unique and imaginative opportunity. It is an opportunity which goes far beyond the mere provision of employment, and opens the way for top nonacademic talent to inject a great new wisdom into the academic process.

But for the academic institutions, the internship component presents a formidable challenge. It demands a new kind of flexibility in the staging of the academic program—a somewhat different approach to the sources of knowledge— and a far more reasonable view of the use of urban talent for the higher-educational task. It requires a fresh approach to what the "campus" is, who a faculty should be, and how knowledge and wisdom may best be organized for the purposes of teaching and research.

FIFTH: There are many different ways to organize and present knowledge and wisdom within a formal-educational framework. There are many different places and situations which can be constructed to accommodate the teacher-learner relationship. Unfortunately, our colleges and universities have overcommitted themselves to one rigid frame.

The subject matter of a discipline is divided up into courses. The courses are dominated by the credit-hour value. The credit-hour course inevitably means sitting in the class for one or two hours.

The classroom student-teacher confrontation presents as many problems as it solves. The encounter between the key people is necessarily stilted. The subject matter presented is necessarily segmented. The relationships among the various fields of knowledge are invariably subverted. Under these circumstances, the lecture inevitably counts for too much. Note taking easily can become an obsession. Testing for marks almost always becomes the exclusive and ultimate criterion of achievement. The situation is tight, inflexible, tense, often damaging to many people who simply do not learn best in such an environment, and equally damaging to many fields of knowledge which do not fit comfortably into the mold.

The higher one goes in the existing academic scale, the greater the number of safety valves built into the course/classroom machine to let out the built-up steam. At the graduate level the somewhat less formal seminar, the self-directed study program, and the library may play bigger roles. But these resources are squandered at the lower levels, where they could be even more effective.

The issue here is really not whether the lecture, the classroom, the discussion group, the library are better or worse than something else. The issue is the bureaucratization of the learning environment and the relationships imposed upon scholars by a mechanically contrived setting which has less and less connection to the condition of knowledge in many fields.

The reorganization of knowledge around *problems* makes a great deal of sense for the purposes of education in the urban black community. To the extent that knowledge can be related to events and experiences which are known to the students, its relevance is tremendously enhanced and the motivation to learn, strengthened. The problem orientation of knowledge will not, of course, terminate the necessity for a rigorous, highly disciplined approach to subjects in various fields at various times. But it necessarily leads to loosening up the situation and to pacing things differently. It will reduce the value of the credit-hour currency, forcing it to serve the only limited purpose it should—keeping score for those parts of the system which require it. It will undermine the centrality of the classroom forum and compel more frequent and less formal engagements with teachers and fellow students. It will involve students and teachers in looking at complex tapestries of knowledge, fields artfully interwoven as any complicated, real problem interweaves different subjects. And it will expose the student immediately to the sensitive, relevant connections between thinking and acting, between the acquisition and use of intelligence and the resolution of matters that count.

The reorganization of curricula around problems magnifies the importance of experience in the educational process. Planning the environments in which students should be immersed becomes a very basic part of curriculum planning. In the new college three such environments are primary: (1) the college setting itself (the ongoing life of teachers, students, and members of the community working together in the pursuit of knowledge); (2) the work environment into which the student is placed by the internship program (banks, offices of government, museums, schools, hospitals, parks, stores, courtrooms, etc.); and (3) the community in which the college is located.

In many ways the immediate community is the most relevant field, for in fact it is the student's home, the home in which he lives as well as learns. To connect the student's formal education to the ongoing dynamics of his community —especially when his community is black and urban—is perhaps the most significant educational result a college in the city could achieve. Through such a connection, the city itself—the spirit and meaning of it—may in fact become the student's true home.

SIXTH, and perhaps most important of all: *The most squandered, underutilized, misused, and abused educational*

resource in this country's colleges and universities is students.
This assertion is made with full knowledge that it is perhaps
the most controversial sentence written in this book—which,
if true, is simply symptomatic of how far the decay has gone
in the higher-educational system of the overlive society.

Perhaps the most important consequence of the technological success and the new knowledge is the extent to which
they have dramatically expanded everybody's ignorance.
Given what there is to know and to do now, nobody can say
that he knows or is doing very much. About the only significant comparisons to be made between today's college student
and his teacher are these: usually the student is an adult
somewhat younger than his teacher; each knows something
the other doesn't; and both are in deep trouble. In each of
these three categories, who holds the advantage is a moot
point.

There has been a sad confusion about the relationship between the discipline implied by the student-teacher connection—a discipline implicitly hierarchal for some purposes, if
not authoritarian—and the basic equality which necessarily
exists between two people, both of whom have a lot to learn
and are compelled to face that together. This confusion has
been magnified by the research and publish-or-perish dogma
which prevails on our campuses. There are an extraordinary
number of campuses in this country where the faculties and
the administrators in charge really think the students are a
bother and a deterrent to the main business of the institution!

At the same time, there is a persuasive body of evidence
establishing the fact that the most bothersome students—
the ones who upset the campus systems the most—generally
are the brightest, measuring brightness in the system's own
terms. There is equally persuasive evidence indicating that
in all of our formal learning systems students have a more
penetrating and enduring educational impact on each other
than their teachers have on them.

In the adult world of learning which a university should

be, everybody is a teacher and everybody is a student. That's the ultimate meaning of a community of scholars. For educational as well as for perfectly legitimate political reasons, the university in the city should plan for and facilitate the opportunity for students to teach each other. And in the college serving the urban black community, the wisdom of the young is even more valuable. For the purposes of that college, a corps of collegians, recruited from a number of other academic places in the city, should be mobilized and paid to serve as tutor-teachers. These young teachers should be chosen on the basis of the relevance of their formal learning, the quality of their prior urban experience, and for their capacity to speak and think in the language of their generation. They should not be selected because they are good imitations of their senior faculties. Those who are chosen should especially be themselves.

Finally, throughout the life of an urban university the students should enjoy the largest possible freedom, the greatest measure of responsibility for their own affairs. Indeed, to the extent that the students can plan and administer their own learning community, they should. Many students now work part time in the admissions, registrar, and other administrative offices of the university. Many need the income from such work. But though they are engaged on many fronts, they are seldom given a share of the policy-making responsibility, the opportunity to review and reorder procedures which most often operate most oppressively on them. These young adults have a special wisdom to contribute to curricular planning, and an invaluable and unique outlook toward the problems of earmarking and deploying the overall wealth of the academic institution.

The *educational* value of student freedom, organized along cooperative lines, is the essence of this proposal. We educators must ask ourselves: What kind of a setting, what network of relationships among human beings achieves the best environment for learning? The authoritarian, patriarchal response to this question is far more difficult to defend in the time of overlive than ever before. The political consequences of the educational position taken are perfectly clear. The leadership of the higher-educational system in this country would go far to restore confidence in itself if it would but clearly recognize the quality and the potentiality of the young adult of college age.

Stony Brook is our main competition, and from what I've seen on my visits there, it's a lily-white campus. They are getting a lot of those very bright, middle-class kids we used to get—should be getting.

And about the students in my own classes, they want to be taught well, they want their degrees, they want to get into the graduate and professional schools. They come here to get the best education they can get. Some of them have told me that they don't want their classes bogged down by those who can't keep up. They don't see this as a race problem.

Sure, they're for social justice and all that. We don't discriminate at this college. We'll take anybody here regardless of race, color, sex or creed—if they can meet our admissions standards. The students on this campus are really interested in high-quality education, and that is what this faculty is interested in, too.

—From a conversation with a member of the
faculty of a senior college in City
University in New York, April 1968

X

Discrimination in
the Search for Excellence

Once we had wooden chalices and golden
priests. Now we have golden chalices and
wooden priests.

RALPH WALDO EMERSON

REAL DIVERSITY and competition have been squeezed out
of the higher-educational system by the overlive success.
To suggest here the substitution of some new monolithic
approach for the old monopoly system would be self-defeat-
ing. The restoration of diversity and competition within the
higher-educational system is an imperative, but only a first
step. The modest proposals with which this argument concludes are but preliminary descriptions of a few destinations
toward which some of our colleges and universities must
soon move.

Most of our campuses and all of our city ghettos are
victims of tyranny. But the tyranny on the campus is largely
self-imposed. It is imposed in the defense of professional
values and habits which contribute to the perpetuation of
the academic ghetto. The recoil of the university from the
idea of the city, the aggressive academic defense of institutional neutrality, the continuing attempt to insulate the
learning process from the volatile, imperative and almost
universal connections between knowledge and survival—all

are vestiges of archaic battle plans for the defense of institutional freedom and academic excellence.

The maintenance of academic excellence is the inner defense, the ultimate rationalization of an educational establishment assaulted on all sides by a society which has achieved technological excellence but has yet to realize its human goals. To let the unqualified "in," to mix sentiment or political expediency with a hardheaded perception of who and where the "real talent" is, to corrupt the prevailing standards of "good" and "bad"—these are the real threats as the academics see them.

These *are* the real threats to the American status quo, not only in higher education, but on all fronts. Who is "qualified" to get "in" to political power in this country? Who is "qualified" to get "in" to the strategic decision-making posts in industry, the professions, the arts? How do we tell who is "qualified"? Are the prevailing standards of "good" and "bad" unassailable? And who is qualified to assail them?

To answer these questions, discriminating judgments must be made about people in a country terribly upset about discrimination.

The American political premise that all men are born equal is matched by the American ideal that the varying talents and potentialities of people will be respected, encouraged and honored. Neither our tradition of universal public education nor the prospect of universal higher education can overlook the reality that people are different, and, in some respects for some purposes, they want to be. Educational opportunity in this country must be addressed to the potential and the consequences of individual differences. It is academic to debate whether talents must be sorted out. But how are they to be sorted out, for what purposes, by whom, and when?

Academic answers to these questions are given at the threshold of the collegiate opportunity, at the preliminary points where the decisions are made determining who gets into college. The award of the degree at the conclusion of the educational experience is supposed to embody another set of critical judgments. Between these two points "excellence" is judged credit hour by credit hour, course by course, grade by grade.

Decisions about admissions rely mainly upon the evaluation of high-school records and performance on college entrance examinations or a composite of the two.

High-school records are as objective as the quality variance among the thousands of public and private secondary schools in the United States—rural, suburban and city. Across the nation, even within a single school system like the one in New York City, it is perilous, to say the least, to generalize about the quality of the facilities, the teachers, the educational programs or the criteria used to evaluate student capacities. The records produced by the failing high schools serving the black communities in our great cities reveal virtually nothing about the realities of the humans they are supposed to serve. And, of course, in the case of those young adults who drop out of these schools, the records are simply inapplicable.*

When colleges establish admission thresholds of earned high-school averages of 80 to 88 or C to B, they are virtually closing their doors to, absolving themselves of responsibility for the advanced education of thousands of young adults about whose talents most of them do not know much. The failure of the lower-educational system is equated with a talent failure.

High performance on college entrance examinations turns

* "A crisis state exists at Boys High. . . . The class of '67 started with 800 in the freshman class. Three years later there were only 380 candidates for graduation. Of these, 283 received general diplomas, 51 academic diplomas, and the other 46 did not graduate." From a special release of the Parent-Community Council of Boys High School in Bedford-Stuyvesant, Brooklyn, New York, May 1968.

upon the acquisition of skills and perceptions requiring the greatest measure of intellectual conformity—upon competence in the English language, the manipulation of number systems, and the storage of factual knowledge which can best be expressed through the language and the number systems. As John Gardner points out, these tests are

> remarkably effective in sorting out students according to their actual and potential performance in the classroom. But even in this context they are far from perfect, and any system of identification of talent which assumes them to be perfect will commit grave mistakes.[40]

These measures of talent take a special view of intelligence, a view which depreciates the relationship between the *identification of self* and the *will to learn*. This relationship is at the crux of the realities of ghetto life, especially for the young. It is also at the very eye of the storms swirling in the minds of some of our brightest young people now enrolled in some of our very best colleges and universities.

The American political commitment deemphasizes the significance of genetic differences, especially among racial and ethnic groupings. The American technological prejudice, the success in the mass production of almost everything, deemphasizes environmental differences. Uniform, controlled environments are either assumed or created in order to produce large numbers of identical things economically.

To achieve the academic results American society seems to want (or needs), our higher-educational system assumes a prior, common, middle-class environmental experience. This assumption serves as a kind of crude enabling act for the basic political commitment, the mass production of the higher learning. To achieve this production economically, a "controlled" environment is created—the academic (the school) "community," at the heart of which is the classroom and the discipline organized there around the meeting of

the student and the teacher. That meeting, the way it is
staged and all that goes into making it possible, is supposed
to demonstrate the basic compatibility between the aristo-
cratic traditions we have borrowed from our European academic ancestors and the qualitative thrust of contemporary
American middle-class society. Our campuses are planned to
receive middle-class students. Our educational programs are
planned to produce middle-class citizens. Our universities
are planned compromises between an élitist academic inheritance and the exigencies of a society whose survival demands large numbers of highly educated people.

The academic system we have created operates reasonably
well within the context of the goals for which it has been
planned. It produces prodigiously the talent required to staff
American society the way it now is. It insures (or at least
until recently it has insured) the perpetuation of itself.

But our higher-educational system falters when confronted
with (1) a clientele which has not shared the American
middle-class experience and/or (2) is in serious disagreement with fundamental premises upon which such an experience depends. To such clienteles the system appears to make
discriminations unjustly or unwisely—in the classrooms
where formal learning is staged, on the campus where a
very special version of community life is rigged, and at the
thresholds where decisions are made determining who is
kept out. In these cases, the system operates to keep out
those who may want in, who may possess the capacity to
conquer the system within its own terms, but who have been
denied an earlier opportunity to develop that capacity; or
it tends to suppress any serious challenge to its own terms.
In either event, the devices most widely used now to determine who is kept out emphasize those very cultural and
social conditions most often absent in the ghetto.

Collegiate grading systems are at once both arbitrary and
frivolous. They vary from college to college, from department to department, from undergraduate to graduate, and

from teacher to teacher. Alphabetical or numerical, these grading systems are crude and gross measurements of actual performance or of individual change and progress. In both the lower and the higher systems, grades are primarily negative rather than positive indices. Consequently, students who are most distinctive, who fit into the system least readily— the very gifted or those confronting the most difficult problems of self-identification—these students are usually told the least about themselves and their capacities by the grades.

Usually the problem-solving devices used as a basis for obtaining the grades presume that the "problems" have definite answers—that there are "right" and "wrong" solutions to the problems posed. Most of the problems of human existence and intellectual life are not this way. There are no "right" or "wrong" solutions to painting a picture, enduring the realities of a job, nurturing a marriage, or constructing a scientific hypothesis. There are no "right" or "wrong" solutions to a Korea or a Vietnam. There are only events requiring people to think, to be in the hope of becoming.

College degrees can mean no more or less than the meaning of the tests of excellence which start the whole process and the quality-control devices used during it. The degree does not say: This student was admitted on the basis of unusually high performance in the Cedar Falls, Iowa, high school or on the college entrance exams. It does not say: This student got an A— in a third-year history course or a C+ on a fourth-year biology test, and that he took pot as a sophomore and was a star basketball player as a senior. The degree simply says: This student, having been admitted, has performed successfully in terms of the intervening systems imposed upon him. Having passed the tests and more or less kept out of trouble, he should now be prepared to enter society (educated) or to conform to the rigors of the graduate record exams and the academic programs pursuant thereto.

Most students change a great deal between admission and

graduation because or in spite of the planned educational happenings in between. But the degree reveals little about these changes. Society puts a value on the possession of the degree, and thus builds into its own value structure the stilted values upon which many college programs are built.

The mastery of many fields of knowledge implies its own standards of excellence. Frequently a university may assemble a faculty which understands these standards and has a capacity to impart them to others. Particular departments within large institutions are often truly centers for learning. Sometimes a single teacher who understands may be enough.

But all too often, when our academic institutions speak of the pursuit or the maintenance of excellence, they mainly mean their own version of their own overall *institutional* excellence. In these cases the development and cultivation of the excellence of individuals is subservient to the maintenance of "objective" institutional standards. It is not the excellence of individual educational programs which is measured; it is the excellence of the student's participation in these presumably objective, immutable and "excellent" programs which is measured. Thus, when the faculty of a college says it is unwilling to tamper with its existing admission criteria (geared to its own programs), that it does not want to run the risk of "watering down" the "excellence" of its ongoing programs, it is really declaring its unwillingness to change, its resistance to the significant educational challenges of our time, and its conviction that it is doing the best that it can—even if it hasn't faced in a decade or more the question of what the "best" is.

It is perfectly clear that the ability to conceptualize and express oneself in the English language and to master the rudiments of the number systems upon which our science and technology depend is essential to success in American life. But it is also perfectly clear against the backdrop of race discrimination and the failure of lower-educational systems that the opportunity for success is denied to many young adults who have the innate capacity to learn what is necessary.

It is perfectly clear that our own ideals compel us to define an "educated man" in terms going far beyond those skills and talents needed for economic survival. But it is also perfectly clear that, in planning advanced education for young adults, we do not respect and honor these terms sufficiently.

Some may still deplore the prospect of universal higher education in our country. But the American commitment on this front has gone beyond the point of no return. Formal learning beyond the age of eighteen is necessary now and will become more necessary in the future. The political, cultural and social values we have read into the possession of a college degree run deep. They have become as much a part of our scene as a middle-class standard of living, and indeed are linked in the popular mind to the achievement of that standard.

Our colleges and universities stress far too much the measurement of human talents at the threshold of the formal learning experience. They concentrate far too little upon the meaning and quality of the human results produced at the terminal points and the evaluation of their own programs in between. As we enter the period of universal higher education in the United States, these emphases must change.

Judgments about quality always involve discrimination. The question of academic excellence raises the same basic issue which besets every other dimension of American life: On what grounds does discrimination make sense now? In our zeal to accommodate the ongoing needs of an overlive society, have we produced educational systems and programs which in fact homogenize individual differences and segregate talents in a manner subversive both of national goals and of sound educational practice? We need not abandon what we now do well in order to correct our obvious failures. "Whether individual differences in ability are innate or are due to environmental differences, we must deal with them imaginatively and constructively."[41]

The traditional views of academic excellence are most challenged on the campuses in the cities. The cities are producing the conditions and the talents to which the university's traditional ways and standards apply most awkwardly. Clark Kerr says that "today's urban universities are less involved in urban problems than they were in the 1930's. They are in the urban setting, but not of it." This is not a neutral position to be in. To be in the urban setting but not of it is to be against it. Our colleges and universities have taken a very aloof position on the great urban issues. But now aloofness is no longer possible. Out of necessity these institutions are compelled to change. They are changing in order to rescue themselves, in order to be what they are supposed to be.

Overlive creates a profound division within all Americans of all classes. It divides the part of us which believes in and aspires to the American promise from the part of us which participates in, accepts, tolerates and is dominated by what America actually is.

This deep split in American life transcends black and white, rich and poor, educated and ignorant, slum and suburb. Elements of class warfare are present, but *every* American must decide in his own way whether pursuing the material pot at the end of America's golden rainbow is the ultimate good. The slumdweller approaches this decision from a wholly different set of circumstances than the suburbanite, but both must make essentially similar moral decisions. The affluent and their institutional instruments—universities, for example—have for too long chosen not to confront the issue. They have paid it lip service on occasion, but in practice they have ignored it. By doing nothing they have taken their stand. But now that stand is in the open, the meaning of it more clearly understood.

Doing nothing is a passive decision, but on the other side of the overlive spectrum the message is loud and clear. Passive decisions about important issues are virtually precluded for the poor and the black in the overlive society. Issues here must be confronted in order to survive, which is why the test of the American Way is being made on the streets of our city ghettos. How we meet the test will determine the future not only of the ghettos and the blacks, but of all of us.

Historically none of this should be surprising. The affluent and those who feel they are within the reach of affluence, have always been too busy playing by the rules of the game to be much concerned about other things.

Black America is the testing ground for our moral crisis. There is no more prevailing American tradition than having our black people do the dirty, messy, difficult business of society. In those institutions where people can be hurt—in bad schools, in inferior and demeaning occupations, in wars —the black people have manned the front lines.

But now, by the simple assertion of themselves, by the declaration of their human being, the black people have moved us all to the front lines, to the ultimate meanings of white America, to the realities of America. On the front lines no one, no institution, no profession can be "in it . . . but not of it." We must think our way through it, calmly, but with conviction. Finally, we must dedicate ourselves passionately to the translation of what we think and know into new actions.

Bibliographical Notes

I. OVERLIVE

1. Max Lerner, *The Age of Overkill* (New York: Simon and Schuster, 1962), p. 23.
2. *Ibid.*, p. 24.
3. Statement of the Black Caucus attending the annual meeting of the National Committee for Support of the Public Schools, Washington, D.C., March 19, 1968.

II. THE UNIVERSITY AND THE ANTI-CITY

4. *The Long Island University Magazine*, Vol. 1, No. 3 (Alumni Association, 1967), p. 37.
5. Quoted by Stewart Alsop in "Mr. Genocide," *Saturday Evening Post*, September 9, 1967, p. 14.
6. Sir Eric Ashby, *Technology and the Academics* (New York: St. Martin's Press, 1958), p. 68.
7. James Perkins, *The University in Transition* (Princeton, N.J.: Princeton University Press, 1966), p. 38.

III. POWER AND THE UNIVERSITY

8. Gertrude Stein, "American Education and Colleges," *The New York Herald Tribune*, March 16, 1935.
9. Sir Eric Ashby, *op. cit.*, p. 3.
10. Edward H. Levi, "Commitment to Reason," *Chicago Sun-Times*, November 26, 1967, Section Two, pp. 1-3.
11. Charles Homer Haskins, *The Rise of Universities* (9th ed.; Ithaca, N.Y.: Cornell University Press, 1966), pp. 8-9.
12. *Ibid.*, p. 11.
13. *Ibid.*, pp. 21-24.

14. Lewis Mumford, *The City in History* (New York: Harcourt, Brace & World, Inc., 1961), p. 276.

15. "Rise in Higher Educational Cost in Last Forty Years," *The New York Times*, September 17, 1967, Section E, p. 11.

16. Lewis Mumford, *op. cit.*, p. 277.

17. James Perkins, *op. cit.*, p. 27.

18. "The University at the Service of Society," reprint from the *1966–67 Annual Report of the Trustees* of the Carnegie Foundation for the Advancement of Teaching (New York City), p. 8.

19. Clark Kerr, *The Uses of the University* (New York: Harper & Row, 1963), p. vii.

IV. THINKING IN AN ACTION WORLD

20. Albert Einstein, *Essays in Science* (New York: Philosophical Library, 1934), p. 114.

21. James Perkins, *op. cit.*, p. 51.

22. Earl C. Kelley, "The Teaching of Controversial Issues," *A Review of General Semantics*, Vol. 19, No. 2 (July, 1962), p. 133. (For an elaboration of point.)

23. John F. Kennedy, "Commencement Address to the Yale Graduating Class," *The New York Times*, June 12, 1962, p. 20.

V. ACTING IN AN ACADEMIC WORLD

24. Grayson Kirk, "Student Freedoms and Responsibilities in American Higher Education," address at the Greater Hartford Forum, Hartford, Connecticut, November 3, 1965.

25. "Pusey Defends Neutral Stance in Social Issues," *The Chronicle of Higher Education*, March 11, 1968, p. 8.

26. Clark Kerr, *op. cit.*, p. 36.

27. James Perkins, *op. cit.*, p. 57.

28. *Quoted in Time*, Education Section, April 14, 1967.

29. Richard Hofstadter and C. DeWitt Hardy, *The Development and Scope of Higher Education* (New York: Columbia University Press, 1952), p. 130.

30. Ben Shahn, *The Shape of Content* (Cambridge, Mass.: Harvard University Press, 1957), pp. 53–72.

VI. LEARNING AND SURVIVAL

31. "Being Trained for Unemployment," *The New York Times*, December 10, 1967, Section E., p. 6.

32. "Percy Tells Republicans: Get Rid of the Stuffy Image," *The New York Post*, October 13, 1967, p. 7.

33. Hugh Philip, "Education in the Metropolis," *Centennial Study and Training Programme on Metropolitan Problems* (Paper No. 8; Toronto, Canada: Bureau of Municipal Research, March 1967), p. 5.

34. "Bonn Urged To Curb College Admissions," *The New York Times*, March 3, 1968.

VII. FREEDOM NOW?

35. P. L. Ford (Editor), *The Writings of Thomas Jefferson* (1894), Vol. IV, pp. 226–27.

36. "Rusk Denies Fear of Intellectuals," *The New York Times*, October 13, 1967, p. 15.

VIII. SOMETHING FOR EVERYBODY IS NOT ENOUGH

37. Horace M. Kallen, *City Planning and the Idea of the City* (Brooklyn, N.Y.: Long Island University Press, 1966).

38. "Proposal Abstract," Training Resources for Youth, Inc. (New York City, June 1965), p. 2.

39. *Ibid.*, p. 3.

X. DISCRIMINATION IN THE SEARCH FOR EXCELLENCE

40. John Gardner, *Excellence* (New York: Harper & Brothers, 1961), p. 49.
41. *Ibid.*, p. 58.

Index

DATE DUE

NOV 2 4 19			